Behind the Code of David Patterson

RISC's Architect – Unauthorized

Amina Hernandez

ISBN: 9781779699930
Imprint: Telephasic Workshop

Contents

Introduction

The Rise of David Patterson

Early Years and Childhood Dreams

David Patterson was born in the heart of the Silicon Valley, a place that would come to symbolize innovation and technological advancement. His childhood was marked by a unique blend of curiosity and creativity, traits that would later define his career as a pioneering computer architect. Growing up in a family that valued education and intellectual pursuits, David was encouraged to explore his interests from an early age.

The Influence of a Technologically Rich Environment

The 1960s and 1970s were transformative years for technology, and living in California during this period provided David with a front-row seat to the burgeoning tech revolution. His father, an engineer, often brought home gadgets that fascinated young David. From early calculators to the first home computers, these devices ignited a spark in him. He would spend hours disassembling and reassembling these machines, driven by an insatiable curiosity about how they worked.

Early Interests in Science and Mathematics

David's passion for programming was complemented by a strong foundation in mathematics and science. He excelled in these subjects at school, often participating in math competitions and science fairs. His teachers recognized his exceptional aptitude and encouraged him to pursue advanced studies. It was during this time that David encountered his first real programming language:

BASIC. The thrill of writing code and seeing it come to life on the screen was exhilarating and set the stage for his future endeavors.

The First Encounter with Programming

At the age of twelve, David had his first encounter with a computer at a local community center. It was a time when computers were not as ubiquitous as they are today, and access was limited. However, the moment he typed his first command and watched the computer respond was transformative. This experience was akin to the moment a musician feels the power of their instrument for the first time. The simplicity of the command line and the immediate feedback it provided were intoxicating. David spent countless hours at the center, learning everything he could about programming.

Dreaming Big: The Influence of Science Fiction

David was not just a tech enthusiast; he was also an avid reader. Science fiction novels captivated his imagination and expanded his horizons. Authors like Isaac Asimov and Arthur C. Clarke painted vivid pictures of future technologies and their impact on society. These stories fueled David's dreams of becoming a computer scientist who could change the world. He often envisioned a future where computers would be integrated into everyday life, enhancing the human experience in ways previously thought impossible.

The Formation of Core Values

As David navigated his early years, he began to form core values that would guide him throughout his life. Curiosity, perseverance, and a commitment to learning became his guiding principles. He believed that technology should be accessible to everyone, and this belief would later manifest in his advocacy for open-source computing. His childhood experiences shaped not only his technical skills but also his ethical framework, emphasizing the importance of using technology for the greater good.

A Vision for the Future

By the time David reached high school, his dreams had crystallized into a clear vision: he wanted to be at the forefront of computer science. He envisioned a future where computers could perform complex tasks, revolutionizing industries and improving lives. This ambition was not just about personal success; it was about contributing to a technological landscape that could empower individuals and communities alike.

In summary, David Patterson's early years were characterized by a deep curiosity about technology, a passion for programming, and a vision for the future that transcended personal ambition. These formative experiences laid the groundwork for his groundbreaking contributions to computer architecture and his enduring legacy in the tech industry. As we delve deeper into Patterson's life, it becomes evident that the dreams and aspirations of his youth were merely the beginning of a remarkable journey that would shape the future of computing.

Conclusion

In conclusion, the early years of David Patterson were not just a backdrop to his later achievements; they were a crucial part of his story. The influences of his family, environment, and personal interests converged to create a unique individual poised to make a significant impact on the world of technology. As we continue to explore Patterson's life and work, we will see how these early dreams evolved into groundbreaking innovations that changed the computing landscape forever.

Discovering a Passion for Programming

David Patterson's journey into the world of programming was not merely a career choice; it was the unfolding of a passion that had been ignited during his formative years. Growing up in a household that valued curiosity and learning, Patterson found himself drawn to the mysteries of technology from an early age. This fascination would ultimately guide him towards the realm of computer science, where he would leave an indelible mark.

The First Encounter

Patterson's first encounter with programming came at the age of twelve when he stumbled upon a book about BASIC programming language in his school library. The book, with its simple syntax and interactive nature, opened a door to a new world. He recalls, "It felt like magic, being able to tell the computer what to do and seeing it respond." This initial experience was a catalyst, sparking a desire to learn more about how computers worked and how he could manipulate them to create his own programs.

The Influence of Early Technology

The early 1970s were a transformative time for technology, with the advent of personal computers on the horizon. Patterson was captivated by the idea of writing code that could produce tangible results. He began experimenting with small programs, creating simple games and utilities. This hands-on experience allowed him to grasp fundamental programming concepts, such as loops, conditionals, and variables. The exhilaration of debugging a program or optimizing code became a source of joy for him, reinforcing his desire to delve deeper into the field.

Academic Exploration

As Patterson progressed through high school, he sought out opportunities to expand his programming skills. Enrolling in advanced mathematics and science courses, he excelled in subjects that required logical reasoning and problem-solving. It was during this time that he discovered the beauty of algorithms—the step-by-step procedures for solving problems. For instance, he learned about the Euclidean algorithm for finding the greatest common divisor (GCD) of two numbers, which not only showcased the elegance of mathematical logic but also its practical applications in programming.

$$\text{GCD}(a,b) = \begin{cases} b\&\text{if } a = 0 \\ \text{GCD}(b \mod a, a)\&\text{otherwise} \end{cases} \tag{1}$$

This equation exemplifies how programming can be used to implement mathematical concepts effectively. Patterson's fascination with algorithms would later play a crucial role in his research and contributions to computer architecture.

The Spark of Innovation

During his high school years, Patterson also participated in a summer program at a local university, where he was introduced to more advanced programming languages such as Pascal and C. It was here that he encountered the concept of structured programming, which emphasized the importance of clear, logical code organization. This experience not only honed his coding skills but also instilled in him a sense of discipline and creativity in software design.

The thrill of creating programs that could solve complex problems or simulate real-world scenarios solidified Patterson's passion for programming. He recalls working on a project that involved developing a simulation of a traffic system, where he implemented algorithms to manage traffic flow. This project was not just an academic exercise; it was a glimpse into the potential of technology to impact society positively.

Challenges Faced

However, the path to discovering his passion was not without challenges. Patterson faced moments of frustration, particularly when debugging complex code or grappling with concepts that seemed insurmountable. Yet, these challenges only fueled his determination. He learned that perseverance and a willingness to learn from mistakes were essential traits for any programmer. Each obstacle became an opportunity for growth, shaping his approach to problem-solving.

A Community of Innovators

As Patterson's skills grew, he began to connect with like-minded peers who shared his enthusiasm for programming. This burgeoning community of innovators provided a supportive environment where ideas could be exchanged, and collaboration flourished. They would often gather to work on projects, share knowledge, and inspire each other to push the boundaries of what was possible with technology.

The Decision to Pursue Technology

By the time he graduated high school, Patterson was certain of his career path. He made the pivotal decision to pursue a degree in electrical engineering and computer science at the University of California, Berkeley. This choice would set the stage for his groundbreaking work in computer architecture and the development of the Reduced Instruction Set Computer (RISC) architecture.

In conclusion, David Patterson's discovery of his passion for programming was a multifaceted journey marked by curiosity, exploration, and resilience. From his early encounters with BASIC to his academic pursuits at Berkeley, each experience contributed to shaping his identity as a visionary in the tech world. This passion would not only drive his personal achievements but also inspire countless others to explore the limitless possibilities of programming and technology.

Academic Journey and Pioneering Research

David Patterson's academic journey began at the prestigious **University of California, Berkeley**, where he enrolled in the early 1970s. This was a transformative period not only for Patterson but also for the field of computer science as a whole. Berkeley was a hotbed of innovation, and it was here that Patterson would lay the groundwork for what would become a revolutionary approach to computer architecture.

Theoretical Foundations of Computer Architecture

Patterson's early academic pursuits were deeply rooted in the theoretical underpinnings of computer science. He was particularly influenced by the works of pioneers such as **John von Neumann**, whose architecture laid the foundation for modern computing. The *von Neumann architecture* describes a system where a single memory space holds both instructions and data, leading to the concept of a stored-program computer. However, as computers evolved, the limitations of this architecture became apparent, particularly in terms of performance and efficiency.

In his research, Patterson sought to address these limitations by exploring alternative architectures. He was inspired by the idea that simplifying the instruction set could lead to more efficient processing. This concept would later become the cornerstone of his groundbreaking work on **Reduced Instruction Set Computing** (RISC).

Pioneering Research on RISC

Patterson's seminal paper, co-authored with his colleague **John L. Hennessy**, introduced the RISC architecture, which proposed a simplified set of instructions that could be executed in a single clock cycle. This idea was rooted in the observation that many complex instructions were rarely used in practical applications. By focusing on a smaller set of frequently used instructions, RISC aimed to improve performance and efficiency.

The RISC architecture can be mathematically represented by the following equation:

$$\text{Performance} = \frac{\text{Number of Instructions Executed} \times \text{Cycles per Instruction}}{\text{Execution Time}} \tag{2}$$

Here, the goal was to minimize the *Cycles per Instruction* (CPI) by reducing the complexity of the instructions themselves. This reduction allowed for more efficient use of the CPU pipeline, a technique that involves overlapping the execution of multiple instructions to increase throughput.

Challenges and Breakthroughs

Patterson's research was not without its challenges. When he first proposed the RISC architecture, it faced skepticism from established industry leaders who were deeply invested in the more complex **Complex Instruction Set Computing (CISC)** architectures. The debate between RISC and CISC was fierce, with proponents of each side arguing their merits.

One of the critical breakthroughs in Patterson's research was the demonstration that RISC could outperform CISC architectures in specific applications. This was particularly evident in the context of *compiler optimization*, where RISC's simpler instructions allowed for more effective use of registers and memory. The following equation illustrates the efficiency gain:

$$\text{Efficiency Gain} = \frac{\text{RISC Execution Time}}{\text{CISC Execution Time}} < 1 \tag{3}$$

Through rigorous testing and validation, Patterson and his team showcased that RISC processors could deliver higher performance at lower power consumption, a crucial consideration as the demand for mobile and embedded systems grew.

Collaborative Efforts and Industry Impact

Patterson's collaboration with John Hennessy was instrumental in the development of the RISC architecture. Together, they published influential papers and worked on projects that would shape the future of computing. Their joint efforts culminated in the creation of the **MIPS architecture**, which became one of the first commercially successful RISC processors.

The impact of Patterson's work extended beyond academia into the broader tech industry. Major companies, including **Apple**, **IBM**, and **Cisco**, adopted RISC principles in their designs, leading to a significant shift in how processors were developed. The RISC architecture influenced the design of modern processors, which often incorporate RISC principles to achieve higher efficiency and performance.

Legacy and Recognition

Patterson's pioneering research on RISC earned him numerous accolades and recognition within the computing community. He received several awards, including the **IEEE Medal of Honor** and the **ACM Turing Award**, which is often regarded as the "Nobel Prize of Computing." These honors reflect not only his contributions to computer architecture but also his role in shaping the future of technology.

In summary, David Patterson's academic journey and pioneering research on RISC architecture have left an indelible mark on the field of computer science. His innovative thinking and collaborative spirit have inspired generations of engineers and researchers, ensuring that his legacy will continue to influence the evolution of computing for years to come.

The Birth of the RISC Architecture

In the early 1980s, the landscape of computer architecture was dominated by Complex Instruction Set Computing (CISC) architectures, characterized by their rich instruction sets and intricate addressing modes. However, David Patterson, with his visionary approach, began to challenge the status quo, advocating for a new paradigm that would fundamentally change the way processors were designed and operated. This marked the birth of the Reduced Instruction Set Computing (RISC) architecture, a revolutionary concept that emphasized simplicity and efficiency.

Theoretical Foundations of RISC

At its core, RISC is based on the idea that a processor's instruction set should be streamlined to improve performance and efficiency. The foundational theory behind RISC can be summarized by the following principles:

- **Simplicity:** RISC architectures utilize a smaller number of instructions, each designed to execute in a single clock cycle. This simplicity allows for faster instruction decoding and execution.

- **Load/Store Architecture:** RISC separates memory access from computation. Only load and store instructions can access memory, while all other operations occur between registers. This reduces memory access latency and enhances performance.

- **Fixed-Length Instructions:** RISC employs a uniform instruction length, typically 32 bits. This regularity simplifies instruction fetching and decoding, leading to more efficient pipelining.

- **Emphasis on Compiler Optimization:** RISC architectures rely heavily on optimizing compilers to generate efficient code that maximizes the use of the simplified instruction set, allowing for better performance without complex hardware.

These principles were not just theoretical; they were grounded in practical observations about the limitations of existing architectures.

Identifying Problems in CISC Architectures

Before the advent of RISC, CISC architectures, such as Intel's x86 and the Motorola 68000 series, faced several challenges:

- **Complexity:** CISC processors had extensive instruction sets, leading to complicated decoding logic. This complexity resulted in longer execution times and increased power consumption.
- **Variable Instruction Length:** CISC instructions could vary in length, complicating instruction fetching and pipelining. This variability hindered the ability to execute multiple instructions simultaneously.
- **Inefficient Use of Registers:** CISC architectures often relied on memory for operations, leading to frequent memory accesses that slowed down execution. The limited number of registers exacerbated this issue.

Patterson's goal was to address these issues by creating a processor architecture that was not only efficient but also scalable for future advancements in technology.

The Development of RISC at Berkeley

In 1981, David Patterson, along with his team at the University of California, Berkeley, began developing the RISC architecture as part of a research project. The initiative aimed to create a new type of microprocessor that would embody the principles of RISC. The project, known as the RISC I, was a prototype that demonstrated the feasibility of the RISC approach.

The RISC I processor was notable for its:

- **Simplified Instruction Set:** RISC I featured a reduced instruction set that focused on common operations, allowing for rapid execution.
- **Register-Based Operations:** With a larger number of general-purpose registers, RISC I minimized memory access, improving overall performance.

- **Single-Cycle Execution:** Most instructions were designed to execute in one clock cycle, which was a significant departure from CISC architectures.

The success of RISC I laid the groundwork for subsequent iterations, including RISC II, which further refined the architecture and introduced pipelining—a technique that allowed multiple instruction phases to be processed simultaneously, thereby enhancing throughput.

Pioneering Research and Recognition

As the RISC architecture evolved, Patterson and his team published their findings, garnering attention from both academia and industry. The seminal paper titled "Reduced Instruction Set Computer Architecture" co-authored by Patterson, was instrumental in spreading awareness of the RISC philosophy. This paper highlighted the advantages of RISC over CISC and provided a detailed comparison of performance metrics.

The impact of RISC began to reverberate throughout the computing industry. Major companies, including IBM, Sun Microsystems, and MIPS Computer Systems, recognized the potential of RISC and began to adopt its principles in their own processor designs. This adoption marked a significant shift in the industry, as RISC processors became increasingly popular in both workstations and embedded systems.

The Legacy of RISC Architecture

The birth of RISC architecture not only transformed the design of processors but also set the stage for future innovations in computing. The principles established by Patterson and his team continue to influence modern architectures, including ARM and RISC-V, which embody the RISC philosophy in their designs.

In summary, the birth of the RISC architecture was a pivotal moment in the history of computing. David Patterson's vision and relentless pursuit of efficiency led to a revolutionary approach that reshaped the industry. As we delve deeper into Patterson's journey, it becomes evident that the RISC architecture was not merely a technical achievement; it was a testament to the power of innovative thinking and the relentless pursuit of excellence in technology.

Gaining Recognition in the Tech World

David Patterson's journey into the limelight of the tech world was not merely a product of his groundbreaking work on Reduced Instruction Set Computing

(RISC) architecture, but also a reflection of his ability to articulate complex ideas and his commitment to innovation. As he delved deeper into the world of computer architecture, Patterson began to gain recognition for his contributions, leading to a series of pivotal moments that would cement his status as a leading figure in the field.

The Rise of RISC

The RISC architecture, which Patterson co-developed, was a radical departure from the then-dominant Complex Instruction Set Computing (CISC) architectures. This new approach emphasized a smaller set of instructions, which could be executed more quickly and efficiently. The fundamental equation that described the performance improvement can be expressed as:

$$\text{Performance} = \text{Instruction Count} \times \text{Cycles per Instruction} \times \text{Cycle Time} \quad (4)$$

By reducing the cycles per instruction and optimizing the cycle time, RISC processors could achieve higher performance at lower power consumption, a critical factor in the burgeoning mobile and embedded systems markets.

Academic Recognition

Patterson's academic prowess was recognized early in his career. His work at the University of California, Berkeley, alongside his collaborator John L. Hennessy, led to the publication of seminal papers that laid the groundwork for RISC. One of the most notable was the 1981 paper titled "The Case for the RISC," which argued for the advantages of a simplified instruction set. This paper not only sparked interest within academic circles but also caught the attention of industry leaders, leading to invitations to speak at conferences and workshops.

Through these presentations, Patterson showcased the potential of RISC architecture, demonstrating how it could revolutionize computing. He used a combination of theoretical analysis and practical demonstrations, including performance benchmarks that highlighted the efficiency of RISC over CISC. For instance, he presented comparisons of benchmark results, such as the SPEC benchmarks, which illustrated the performance gains achieved through RISC designs.

Industry Impact

As the tech industry began to recognize the benefits of RISC, Patterson's influence grew. Major companies like IBM, Sun Microsystems, and MIPS Computer Systems began to adopt RISC architectures in their products. This shift was not without its challenges, as entrenched CISC architectures were deeply integrated into existing systems. Patterson faced skepticism from traditionalists who argued that the complexity of CISC was necessary for certain applications.

However, Patterson's relentless advocacy for RISC architecture, coupled with the growing body of evidence supporting its effectiveness, led to a gradual acceptance within the industry. The introduction of RISC-based processors, such as the MIPS R2000 and the SPARC architecture, showcased the real-world applicability of Patterson's ideas. These processors not only outperformed their CISC counterparts in many scenarios but also set new standards for power efficiency.

Awards and Honors

Patterson's contributions did not go unnoticed. He received numerous accolades that further solidified his reputation. In 1997, he was awarded the prestigious ACM/IEEE Eckert-Mauchly Award for his pioneering work in computer architecture. This award is given to individuals who have made significant contributions to the field, and Patterson's recognition was a testament to the impact of RISC.

Additionally, he was elected to the National Academy of Engineering in 1998, an honor reserved for those who have made outstanding contributions to engineering. His election highlighted not only his technical achievements but also his role in shaping the future of computing.

Public Engagement and Thought Leadership

Patterson's recognition extended beyond academia and industry; he became a thought leader in the tech community. He was frequently invited to participate in panel discussions and keynote speeches at major technology conferences. His ability to communicate complex ideas in an accessible manner made him a sought-after speaker. Patterson's presentations often included engaging visuals and relatable analogies, allowing audiences to grasp the significance of his work.

Moreover, Patterson authored several influential books, including "Computer Organization and Design," which became a staple in computer science education.

These publications further established him as an authority in the field, reaching both students and professionals eager to learn about computer architecture.

Legacy and Continued Influence

The recognition Patterson gained in the tech world laid the foundation for his enduring legacy. The principles of RISC architecture continue to influence modern computing, as seen in the design of contemporary processors, including those used in smartphones and tablets. The RISC philosophy has also led to the development of RISC-V, an open standard that Patterson championed, promoting accessibility and innovation in computer architecture.

In conclusion, David Patterson's ascent in the tech world was characterized by his innovative contributions, academic recognition, and public engagement. His work not only transformed the landscape of computer architecture but also inspired a new generation of technologists. As the industry continues to evolve, Patterson's influence remains a guiding light, reminding us of the power of creativity and innovation in shaping the future of technology.

Challenges and Controversies

David Patterson's journey to becoming a pioneering figure in computer architecture was not without its challenges and controversies. As he navigated the complex landscape of technology, he encountered numerous obstacles that tested his resolve and shaped his contributions to the field.

Industry Resistance to RISC

One of the most significant challenges Patterson faced was the resistance from established industry players to the Reduced Instruction Set Computer (RISC) architecture. When Patterson and his colleagues at the University of California, Berkeley, introduced the RISC concept in the early 1980s, they proposed a radical shift in how processors were designed. The traditional Complex Instruction Set Computer (CISC) architecture dominated the market, and many industry leaders were skeptical of RISC's potential.

$$\text{Performance} = \frac{\text{Number of Instructions}}{\text{Execution Time}} \tag{5}$$

This equation illustrates the performance metrics that Patterson aimed to improve with RISC. However, the entrenched interests in CISC systems, such as Intel and IBM, viewed RISC as a threat to their business models. Patterson's advocacy for RISC led to a wave of pushback, with critics arguing that the simplified instruction set would lead to inefficiencies and limit the capabilities of processors.

Academic Controversies

In addition to industry resistance, Patterson faced controversies within the academic community. His close collaboration with John L. Hennessy, who later became the president of Stanford University, sparked debates about the ethics of academic partnerships and the commercialization of research. While their joint efforts led to groundbreaking advancements in RISC, some academics questioned whether their focus on industry collaboration compromised the integrity of their research.

Furthermore, Patterson's outspoken nature regarding the importance of open-source technology created friction with colleagues who preferred proprietary systems. His advocacy for open-source solutions in the RISC-V initiative challenged the status quo, leading to heated discussions about intellectual property and the future of computing.

Ethical Dilemmas in Technology

As Patterson's influence grew, so did the ethical dilemmas associated with technological advancements. The rapid evolution of computing technologies raised questions about privacy, data security, and the societal implications of automation. Patterson found himself at the center of discussions about the ethical responsibilities of technologists.

For instance, the rise of machine learning and artificial intelligence brought forth concerns regarding bias in algorithms and the potential for misuse of technology. Patterson's commitment to responsible innovation led him to engage in conversations about how to create inclusive and equitable technologies. He often emphasized the need for diverse teams in tech to mitigate biases and ensure that innovations serve the broader society.

The GPL Revolution and Open Source Advocacy

Patterson's advocacy for open-source technology was met with both enthusiasm and skepticism. While many embraced the idea of making technology accessible to all, others viewed it as a threat to their proprietary business models. The General Public License (GPL) revolution, which promoted open-source software, created a rift in the industry. Patterson's involvement with the RISC-V Foundation, which aimed to democratize processor design, further fueled the controversy.

The RISC-V architecture, which allowed anyone to design and implement RISC processors without licensing fees, faced pushback from established companies that had invested heavily in proprietary architectures. Patterson's vision of an open-source future for computing clashed with the interests of those who sought to maintain control over their technologies.

Public Perception and Media Scrutiny

As Patterson's fame grew, so did the scrutiny from the media. His public persona as a tech guru and visionary attracted attention, but it also exposed him to criticism and misrepresentation. Some media outlets sensationalized his work, portraying him as a controversial figure in the tech industry. This led to a series of interviews and public appearances where Patterson had to clarify his positions and address misconceptions about his contributions to RISC and open-source technology.

The media's portrayal of Patterson often focused on the dramatic aspects of his career, overshadowing the nuanced discussions he sought to promote. This created a tension between his desire to foster meaningful conversations about technology and the sensationalist narratives that dominated public discourse.

Conclusion

In summary, David Patterson's journey was marked by a series of challenges and controversies that shaped his legacy in the computing industry. From resistance to RISC and ethical dilemmas in technology to public scrutiny and media misrepresentation, Patterson navigated a complex landscape that tested his principles and commitment to innovation. His ability to confront these challenges head-on not only solidified his reputation as a tech visionary but also paved the way for future advancements in computer architecture and open-source technology.

Patterson's Impact on the Computing Industry

David Patterson's contributions to the computing industry are nothing short of revolutionary. As the architect of the Reduced Instruction Set Computer (RISC) architecture, Patterson not only reshaped the design of modern processors but also influenced the very way we think about computing efficiency and performance. This section delves into the profound impact Patterson has had on the computing landscape, highlighting key theories, challenges, and examples that illustrate his legacy.

The RISC Revolution

The introduction of RISC architecture marked a pivotal moment in the history of computing. Traditional Complex Instruction Set Computer (CISC) architectures, which relied on a large number of complex instructions, often resulted in inefficient execution and increased power consumption. Patterson's RISC philosophy, on the other hand, emphasized simplicity and efficiency. By reducing the number of instructions and focusing on a smaller set of operations, RISC processors could execute instructions at a higher speed.

The fundamental principle behind RISC can be expressed mathematically in terms of performance improvement:

$$\text{Performance} = \frac{\text{Instructions per second} \times \text{Clock rate}}{\text{Cycles per instruction}} \tag{6}$$

By minimizing the cycles per instruction (CPI) through simplified instruction sets, RISC architecture dramatically improved overall performance. This shift not only led to faster processors but also laid the groundwork for advancements in parallel processing and pipelining techniques.

Influence on Industry Standards

Patterson's work on RISC architecture set new standards for processor design, leading to widespread adoption in both commercial and academic settings. Major technology companies, including IBM, Sun Microsystems, and ARM, embraced RISC principles, resulting in a new generation of high-performance computing systems. The RISC architecture became a reference model for subsequent designs, influencing the development of the SPARC, MIPS, and PowerPC architectures.

Moreover, Patterson's collaboration with John L. Hennessy, which culminated in the publication of the seminal textbook *Computer Organization and Design*, helped disseminate RISC concepts to a broader audience. This text became a foundational resource for computer science curricula worldwide, fostering a new generation of engineers and researchers who would carry the torch of RISC innovation forward.

Addressing Challenges in Computing

Despite its successes, the RISC architecture faced challenges and criticisms, particularly from proponents of CISC designs. Critics argued that RISC's simplicity came at the cost of flexibility and that the reduced instruction set could limit the capabilities of certain applications. In response, Patterson and his colleagues conducted extensive research to demonstrate that RISC could outperform CISC in a variety of contexts, particularly in high-performance computing and embedded systems.

One notable example is the development of the RISC-V architecture, an open standard based on Patterson's principles. RISC-V has gained traction as a flexible and extensible instruction set architecture (ISA) that allows for customization while maintaining the efficiency of RISC. Its open-source nature has fostered collaboration and innovation across the industry, enabling researchers and companies to develop tailored solutions for specific applications.

Legacy and Future Impact

Patterson's impact extends beyond processor architecture; he has also played a crucial role in advocating for open-source technologies and collaborative research. His establishment of the RISC-V Foundation exemplifies his commitment to democratizing access to advanced computing technologies, allowing a diverse range of stakeholders to contribute to the future of computing.

As we look to the future, Patterson's vision for RISC and open-source architecture continues to inspire new generations of technologists. The principles of efficiency, simplicity, and collaboration that he championed are more relevant than ever in an era characterized by rapid technological advancement and increasing demand for sustainable computing solutions.

In conclusion, David Patterson's contributions to the computing industry have left an indelible mark. His pioneering work in RISC architecture not only revolutionized processor design but also laid the foundation for future innovations in computing. As we continue to build upon his legacy, the impact of his vision will resonate for years to come, shaping the way we interact with technology and redefining the boundaries of what is possible in the computing landscape.

The Inspiration for this Unauthorized Biography

In the realm of technology, few figures loom as large as David Patterson, the architect behind the Reduced Instruction Set Computer (RISC) architecture. His journey is not just a tale of circuits and algorithms; it is a narrative that intertwines passion, rebellion, and innovation. This unauthorized biography aims to peel back the layers of Patterson's life and work, offering insights that go beyond the technical achievements to explore the human experiences that shaped him.

The inspiration for this biography stems from a profound recognition of Patterson's influence on modern computing and his often-overlooked personal narrative. In a world where technology evolves at breakneck speed, the individuals who drive these changes often remain in the shadows, their stories untold. Patterson's life is a testament to the power of curiosity and determination, and it is this spirit that fuels the desire to document his journey.

A Personal Connection

As a writer and a technology enthusiast, I found myself drawn to Patterson's story not merely because of his technical accomplishments but due to the personal challenges he faced along the way. Every great innovator encounters obstacles, and Patterson's experiences resonate with anyone who has ever dared to dream big. His early encounters with programming were not without struggle; like many of us, he faced moments of doubt and uncertainty. This biography seeks to illuminate those moments, revealing how they contributed to his resilience and eventual success.

A Reflection of Our Times

The rise of the digital age has brought about a plethora of challenges, from ethical dilemmas surrounding data privacy to the implications of artificial intelligence. Patterson's work in advocating for open-source architecture, particularly with the RISC-V initiative, reflects a critical response to these contemporary issues. This biography serves as a mirror to our times, capturing the essence of a thinker who not only contributed to technological advancement but also engaged in the ethical discourse surrounding it.

The Power of Inspiration

Inspiration is a powerful force, and Patterson's journey has inspired countless individuals to explore the field of computer science. His story exemplifies how one person's passion can ignite a movement, encouraging a new generation of technologists to innovate and challenge the status quo. This biography aims to encapsulate that inspiration, providing a narrative that motivates readers to pursue their own dreams, regardless of the challenges they may face.

A Journey Worth Telling

The decision to write an unauthorized biography is a deliberate one, rooted in the belief that every story deserves to be told, even if it means stepping outside the bounds of official narratives. Patterson's life is rich with experiences that are often overlooked in traditional biographies. By exploring the lesser-known facets of his journey, this book aims to present a more holistic view of the man behind the code.

The Intersection of Technology and Humanity

In the end, this biography seeks to highlight the intersection of technology and humanity. Patterson's contributions to the computing industry are monumental, yet it is his human experiences—the relationships he fostered, the challenges he overcame, and the ethical questions he grappled with—that make his story truly compelling. By delving into these aspects, we can better understand the man who shaped the future of computing and the values that drove him.

In conclusion, the inspiration for this unauthorized biography of David Patterson arises from a desire to celebrate not just his achievements but also the human spirit that fuels innovation. It is a tribute to a visionary who dared to dream and a call to action for those who aspire to leave their mark on the world of technology. As we embark on this journey through Patterson's life, we invite readers to join us in exploring the intricate tapestry of experiences that define one of the most influential figures in modern computing.

$$E = mc^2 \tag{7}$$

This famous equation by Einstein serves as a reminder that the energy of innovation, much like mass, is a powerful force that can change the world. Just as Patterson's work in RISC architecture transformed computing, so too can our individual contributions shape the future.

Why Patterson Deserves to be in the Spotlight

David Patterson is not just a name in the annals of computer science; he is a revolutionary architect whose contributions have fundamentally reshaped the landscape of computing. To understand why Patterson deserves to be in the spotlight, we must delve into the profound impact of his work, the challenges he overcame, and the vision that continues to inspire future generations.

A Pioneer of Computer Architecture

At the heart of Patterson's legacy lies his pioneering work on the Reduced Instruction Set Computer (RISC) architecture. RISC fundamentally changed how processors are designed and operated. By simplifying the instruction set, Patterson enabled faster execution of programs, leading to a significant performance boost in computing systems. The equation that encapsulates the efficiency of RISC can be represented as:

$$\text{Performance} = \frac{\text{Instructions Executed}}{\text{Execution Time}} \tag{8}$$

This equation highlights how reducing the complexity of instructions can lead to faster execution times, a principle that has been embraced by modern processors, including those used in smartphones and tablets today.

Influence on Modern Computing

Patterson's influence extends beyond RISC. His collaborative work with John L. Hennessy led to the development of the RISC-V architecture, an open standard that empowers developers and researchers to innovate freely without the constraints of proprietary systems. RISC-V has gained traction in both academia and industry, demonstrating Patterson's foresight in advocating for open-source principles. The rise of RISC-V can be attributed to its flexibility and adaptability, allowing it to meet the demands of diverse applications, from embedded systems to supercomputers.

Overcoming Challenges and Controversies

Patterson's journey has not been without its challenges. He faced significant resistance from industry giants who were invested in proprietary architectures. His commitment to open-source principles often put him at odds with established norms, leading to controversies that tested his resolve. However, Patterson's ability to navigate these challenges speaks volumes about his character. His advocacy for accessible technology and his role in founding the RISC-V Foundation exemplify his dedication to democratizing computing resources.

A Visionary for the Future

What sets Patterson apart is not just his technical prowess but also his visionary outlook on the future of technology. He understands that the evolution of computing is intrinsically linked to societal progress. Patterson has been vocal about the ethical implications of technology, emphasizing the need for inclusivity and diversity within the tech industry. His efforts to inspire the next generation of technologists through educational initiatives and mentorship programs showcase his commitment to fostering a more equitable technological landscape.

For instance, Patterson's involvement in various outreach programs aims to bridge the gap between underrepresented communities and the tech world. By advocating for increased representation in STEM fields, he is not only shaping the future of technology but also ensuring that it reflects the diversity of society.

Cultural Impact and Public Persona

In addition to his technical achievements, Patterson's charismatic personality and public image have made him a cultural icon in the tech world. His appearances in media, engaging interviews, and collaborations with artists and musicians have helped humanize the image of computer scientists. By cultivating a public persona that resonates with both technical and non-technical audiences, Patterson has made significant strides in shaping how the public perceives the tech industry.

The "Cult of David Patterson" has emerged, demonstrating the profound impact he has had on popular culture. His ability to connect with people beyond the confines of academia highlights the importance of communication and relatability in the tech field.

Conclusion

In conclusion, David Patterson deserves to be in the spotlight not only for his groundbreaking contributions to computer architecture but also for his unwavering commitment to open-source principles, ethical technology, and social impact. His journey embodies the spirit of innovation and resilience, making him a role model for aspiring technologists everywhere. As we continue to navigate the complexities of the digital age, Patterson's vision and legacy will undoubtedly inspire future generations to push the boundaries of what is possible in computing.

What to Expect from the Rest of the Book

In this unauthorized biography of David Patterson, readers will embark on an exhilarating journey through the life and mind of one of computing's most influential figures. The subsequent chapters are meticulously crafted to reveal not just the technical genius behind RISC architecture, but also the human experiences that shaped his career and contributions to the tech industry.

A Deep Dive into Patterson's Early Life

The narrative begins with an exploration of Patterson's formative years, detailing how his childhood dreams and early encounters with technology ignited a passion that would lead to groundbreaking innovations. Expect to uncover stories that highlight the pivotal moments in his youth, such as his first programming experiences and the influence of science fiction on his aspirations. These anecdotes will provide a rich context for understanding the motivations behind his later work.

Academic Excellence and Research Breakthroughs

As we transition into Patterson's academic journey, readers will gain insights into his time at the University of California, Berkeley. This section will delve into his collaborative spirit, showcasing his partnerships with mentors and peers, particularly John L. Hennessy. The narrative will elucidate the challenges he faced while pioneering the RISC architecture, including the technical hurdles and industry skepticism that accompanied his revolutionary ideas.

The RISC Revolution

The heart of the biography will focus on the RISC architecture itself, where readers can expect detailed explanations of its principles and the philosophy that underpins it. The book will illustrate the technical aspects of RISC through equations and diagrams, making complex concepts accessible. For instance, the RISC philosophy can be summarized by the equation:

$$\text{Performance} \propto \frac{\text{Instructions Per Cycle (IPC)} \times \text{Clock Rate}}{\text{Instruction Count}}$$

This equation captures the essence of RISC's design goals: maximizing performance by optimizing instruction execution and minimizing complexity.

Challenges and Controversies

No biography would be complete without addressing the controversies and challenges Patterson faced throughout his career. Expect candid discussions about his advocacy for open-source architecture, including the formation of the RISC-V Foundation. This section will not shy away from the tensions with industry giants and the ethical dilemmas he encountered. Readers will appreciate Patterson's commitment to accessible technology, supported by examples of his collaborations and the pushback he received from established players in the tech landscape.

The Human Element

In the latter chapters, the narrative shifts focus to the human side of David Patterson. Expect to learn about his hobbies, personal relationships, and philanthropic efforts. This section will reveal how Patterson balances his professional aspirations with his personal life, including his contributions to education and humanitarian efforts. Readers will find inspiration in Patterson's moments of vulnerability, reflecting on the importance of mental health in the fast-paced tech industry.

Cultural Impact and Legacy

Finally, the biography will explore Patterson's impact on pop culture and the tech industry at large. Expect to see how his work has influenced popular media, from films to music, and how he has cultivated a public persona that resonates with both tech enthusiasts and the general public. This segment will also discuss the "Cult of David Patterson," examining how his charisma and vision have shaped perceptions of technology in society.

Conclusion

As we conclude this section, readers can look forward to a comprehensive and engaging portrayal of David Patterson's life and legacy. This biography aims not only to inform but also to inspire, shedding light on the complexities of innovation and the human spirit behind the code. With a blend of technical insight, personal anecdotes, and cultural commentary, "Behind the Code of David Patterson" promises to be a captivating read for anyone interested in the evolution of computer science and the remarkable individuals who drive it forward.

Chapter One: A Genius Unveiled

Section One: Roots of Brilliance

The Patterson Family Tree

The roots of David Patterson's brilliance can be traced back through a rich tapestry of familial influences that shaped his early years. Understanding the Patterson family tree is essential to appreciating the environment that fostered David's intellectual growth and passion for technology. This section explores the key figures in his lineage, their contributions, and the values they instilled in him.

Ancestral Background

David Patterson's family history is a mosaic of diverse backgrounds, each contributing to the unique perspectives he would later embody. The Pattersons can trace their ancestry back to early settlers in America, with a lineage that includes educators, engineers, and innovators. This heritage provided a fertile ground for intellectual curiosity and a commitment to learning.

$$\text{Influence} = f(\text{Education}, \text{Innovation}, \text{Values}) \tag{9}$$

Here, the function f represents the cumulative influence of education, innovation, and values passed down through generations. The Pattersons' emphasis on education is evident in the careers chosen by David's ancestors, many of whom were teachers and scholars.

Key Family Members

- **David's Father:** A high school mathematics teacher, he instilled a love for problem-solving and analytical thinking in David from an early age. His father often engaged him in mathematical puzzles and logic games, nurturing David's innate curiosity.

- **David's Mother:** An artist and writer, she encouraged creativity and expression. Her influence is visible in David's ability to think outside the box, a trait that would later manifest in his revolutionary ideas in computer architecture.

- **Grandparents:** Both sets of grandparents were instrumental in David's upbringing. His paternal grandfather was an engineer who worked on early computing machines, while his maternal grandmother was a librarian who fostered a love for literature and knowledge. Their diverse skills and interests provided David with a well-rounded foundation.

Early Influences

The Patterson family gatherings were often filled with discussions about technology, literature, and the arts. This environment not only stimulated David's intellectual growth but also encouraged him to pursue his interests vigorously. Family members frequently shared stories of their professional experiences, which served as inspiration for David's future endeavors.

$$\text{Inspiration} = \sum_{i=1}^{n} \text{Family Stories}_i \tag{10}$$

In this equation, n represents the number of family members who contributed stories, and each story adds to David's inspiration, highlighting the importance of narrative in shaping his ambitions.

The Legacy of Values

The values instilled in David by his family played a crucial role in his development as a programmer and innovator. Key values included:

- **Curiosity:** Encouraged to ask questions and seek answers, David's curiosity drove him to explore the world of computers and programming.

- **Resilience:** The Pattersons faced their share of challenges, and the family's approach to overcoming obstacles taught David the importance of perseverance.
- **Integrity:** A strong moral compass guided the Pattersons, and David learned early on the significance of ethical considerations in technology and innovation.

Conclusion

The Patterson family tree is not merely a collection of names and dates; it is a narrative rich with values, experiences, and influences that shaped David Patterson into the visionary he became. Understanding this familial background provides insight into the motivations and aspirations that fueled his groundbreaking work in computer architecture. As we delve deeper into David's life, it becomes clear that the foundation laid by his family was instrumental in his rise to prominence in the tech world.

Early Indications of Genius

From a young age, David Patterson exhibited a remarkable aptitude for understanding complex concepts, a trait that would later define his illustrious career in computer architecture. The early signs of his genius were not merely coincidental but rather a culmination of his environment, innate curiosity, and the encouragement he received from those around him.

Intellectual Curiosity

Patterson's intellectual curiosity was evident even in his formative years. Growing up in a household that valued education, he was surrounded by books, puzzles, and scientific toys. His parents, both educators, fostered an environment where questions were encouraged, and exploration was celebrated. This nurturing atmosphere laid the groundwork for Patterson's inquisitive nature, prompting him to delve deeper into subjects that piqued his interest.

A notable example of this curiosity was his early fascination with mathematics. At the age of eight, Patterson was introduced to algebraic concepts through a series of engaging workbooks. His ability to grasp these abstract ideas at such a young age was a clear indication of his mathematical prowess. This early engagement with numbers would later serve as a foundation for his work in computer science, where algorithms and logic reign supreme.

Problem-Solving Skills

Patterson's problem-solving skills began to surface during his elementary school years. He often found himself drawn to challenging puzzles and games that required strategic thinking. One of his favorite activities was solving complex mazes, which he approached with a methodical mindset. This ability to analyze problems and devise solutions not only showcased his cognitive abilities but also highlighted his passion for tackling challenges head-on.

An illustrative incident occurred when Patterson was tasked with a science project in the fifth grade. Instead of opting for a straightforward presentation, he decided to build a simple computer using basic electronic components. This project not only demonstrated his understanding of circuitry but also his penchant for innovation. His teacher recognized the ingenuity behind his work, which further fueled Patterson's desire to explore the world of technology.

Early Exposure to Technology

The turning point in Patterson's early life came when he was introduced to computers. At the age of twelve, he encountered a Commodore 64 at a friend's house. The moment he laid hands on the keyboard, a spark ignited within him. He was captivated by the machine's capabilities and spent countless hours experimenting with programming in BASIC. This experience was pivotal, as it marked the beginning of his lifelong relationship with computers.

Patterson's early programming endeavors were not without their challenges. He faced numerous obstacles, such as debugging his code and understanding the intricacies of computer logic. However, these challenges only fueled his determination to learn more. He often stayed up late into the night, driven by an insatiable desire to create and innovate. This relentless pursuit of knowledge would become a hallmark of his character.

Encouragement from Mentors

Throughout his early years, Patterson was fortunate to have mentors who recognized his potential and encouraged him to pursue his interests. One such mentor was his high school mathematics teacher, Mrs. Thompson. She identified Patterson's exceptional aptitude for math and challenged him with advanced topics that were typically reserved for older students. Under her guidance, he excelled in mathematics competitions, earning accolades that further validated his abilities.

Mrs. Thompson's encouragement extended beyond mathematics; she introduced Patterson to programming competitions, where he could showcase his skills. These competitions not only honed his technical abilities but also instilled in him a sense of camaraderie with peers who shared his passion for technology. This supportive network played a crucial role in shaping Patterson's early experiences and solidifying his commitment to a career in computer science.

The Role of Science Fiction

Another significant influence on Patterson's early development was his love for science fiction. He devoured books by authors such as Isaac Asimov and Arthur C. Clarke, which fueled his imagination and inspired him to think beyond the conventional boundaries of technology. These narratives often featured advanced computing systems and artificial intelligence, concepts that resonated with Patterson's aspirations.

In one memorable instance, he was particularly inspired by Clarke's vision of a future where computers played a central role in human society. This vision ignited a desire within Patterson to contribute to the technological advancements that could one day shape the world. His early exposure to science fiction not only broadened his horizons but also motivated him to pursue a path that would ultimately lead to groundbreaking innovations in computer architecture.

Conclusion

In summary, the early indications of David Patterson's genius were evident through his intellectual curiosity, problem-solving skills, exposure to technology, encouragement from mentors, and his love for science fiction. These formative experiences laid the foundation for his future achievements in computer architecture and solidified his place as a pioneering figure in the tech industry. As he navigated through the challenges of his early years, Patterson's innate abilities began to shine, setting the stage for a remarkable journey that would redefine the landscape of computing.

Encouragement from Family and Teachers

David Patterson's journey into the realm of computer science was not solely a product of his innate brilliance; it was significantly shaped by the encouragement he received from both his family and teachers. This section delves into the pivotal role that these figures played in nurturing his passion for technology and innovation.

The Family Foundation

From an early age, the Patterson household was infused with an atmosphere that celebrated curiosity and intellectual exploration. David's parents recognized his burgeoning interest in technology and took proactive steps to foster it. They provided him with access to books about computers and programming, which were rare commodities during the early years of the personal computing revolution. This early exposure laid the groundwork for his future endeavors.

$$\text{Interest}_{\text{technology}} \propto \text{Access}_{\text{resources}} + \text{Support}_{\text{family}} \tag{11}$$

This equation illustrates the relationship between a child's interest in technology and the resources and support available to them. David's parents embodied this equation, ensuring that he had the tools necessary to explore his interests.

The Role of Educators

In addition to familial support, David's teachers played a critical role in his development. They recognized his potential early on and encouraged him to pursue his interests in mathematics and science. One notable figure was his high school mathematics teacher, who introduced him to programming through simple projects that captivated his imagination. This teacher's encouragement was instrumental in helping David see the beauty and logic behind programming languages.

$$\text{Motivation}_{\text{student}} = \text{Inspiration}_{\text{teacher}} + \text{Engagement}_{\text{curriculum}} \tag{12}$$

Here, the motivation of a student can be expressed as a function of the inspiration provided by teachers and the engagement level of the curriculum. David's teachers excelled in both areas, making learning an exciting and rewarding experience.

Mentorship and Guidance

As David transitioned into higher education, mentorship became a significant factor in his academic success. At the University of California, Berkeley, he encountered professors who recognized his talent and took him under their wings. Notably, his relationship with Professor John L. Hennessy would prove to be transformative. Hennessy not only mentored David but also collaborated with him on groundbreaking research projects that would eventually lead to the development of the RISC architecture.

$$\text{Success}_{\text{academic}} \propto \text{Mentorship}_{\text{professors}} \times \text{Collaboration}_{\text{peers}} \tag{13}$$

This equation suggests that academic success is proportional to the quality of mentorship received and the collaborative efforts with peers. David's experience at Berkeley exemplifies this principle, as he thrived in an environment that encouraged collaboration and innovation.

The Power of Encouragement

The encouragement that David received was not merely verbal but manifested in various forms. Family outings to science museums, participation in programming competitions, and attendance at tech conferences provided him with a rich tapestry of experiences that fueled his passion. These activities allowed him to visualize a future in technology and motivated him to pursue it relentlessly.

$$\text{Passion}_{\text{technology}} = \text{Experiences}_{\text{enriching}} + \text{Encouragement}_{\text{positive}} \tag{14}$$

In this context, passion for technology can be seen as the sum of enriching experiences and positive encouragement. David's life was a testament to this equation, as he transformed encouragement into a driving force for his success.

Conclusion

In conclusion, the encouragement from family and teachers played an indispensable role in David Patterson's journey to becoming a pioneer in computer science. Their unwavering support and belief in his abilities provided him with the confidence and motivation needed to explore the world of programming and ultimately revolutionize computer architecture. As we delve deeper into Patterson's life, it becomes evident that the foundation built by those who believed in him was crucial in shaping his path to greatness.

The Spark that Ignited Patterson's Passion for Computers

David Patterson's journey into the world of computers began at a young age, ignited by a series of pivotal moments that shaped his future. Growing up in a family that valued education and creativity, Patterson was encouraged to explore various interests. However, it was the introduction to computers that truly captivated his imagination.

In the early 1970s, during his high school years, Patterson encountered his first computer: a DEC PDP-8. This experience was akin to a spark igniting a fire. The PDP-8, known for its simplicity and affordability, provided a window into the world of programming and computing. This machine, with its blinking lights and whirring sounds, was not just a tool; it was a gateway to a realm where logic and creativity intertwined.

$$\text{Computer Program} = \text{Input} + \text{Processing} + \text{Output} \tag{15}$$

This equation encapsulates the essence of programming, and Patterson quickly grasped the importance of each component. The thrill of writing a program that could manipulate data and produce results was exhilarating. He spent countless hours experimenting with code, often losing track of time as he delved deeper into the mechanics of the machine.

Patterson's fascination was further fueled by the burgeoning world of technology and science fiction. He found inspiration in the works of authors like Isaac Asimov and Arthur C. Clarke, who envisioned futures shaped by advanced technologies. These narratives painted a picture of a world where computers could enhance human capabilities, and Patterson was determined to be part of that vision.

Moreover, the influence of his teachers played a significant role in nurturing his passion. A particularly inspiring computer science teacher introduced him to the concept of algorithms and problem-solving techniques. The teacher emphasized the idea that programming was not just about writing code; it was about thinking critically and creatively to solve complex problems. This approach resonated deeply with Patterson, who began to see programming as both an art and a science.

As Patterson honed his skills, he faced challenges that tested his resolve. Early programming languages, such as FORTRAN and BASIC, presented steep learning curves, and debugging code was often a frustrating endeavor. Yet, each obstacle only fueled his determination to master the craft. He embraced the iterative process of coding—writing, testing, and refining—understanding that failure was an integral part of learning.

$$\text{Success} = \text{Effort} + \text{Learning from Failure} \tag{16}$$

This equation became a mantra for Patterson, guiding him through the ups and downs of his programming journey. He learned to appreciate the value of persistence and resilience, qualities that would serve him well in his future endeavors.

The combination of early exposure to computers, the influence of inspiring mentors, and a relentless pursuit of knowledge set Patterson on a path toward greatness. By the time he enrolled at the University of California, Berkeley, his passion for computers had blossomed into a full-fledged obsession. He was ready to dive into the world of computer architecture, where he would eventually make groundbreaking contributions that would change the landscape of computing forever.

In conclusion, the spark that ignited David Patterson's passion for computers was a confluence of experiences: the first encounter with the PDP-8, the influence of science fiction, the guidance of dedicated teachers, and the challenges he faced along the way. These elements combined to create a fervent desire to explore the limitless possibilities of technology, setting the stage for a remarkable career that would leave an indelible mark on the computing industry.

Patterson's First Encounter with Programming

David Patterson's journey into the realm of programming began in an unexpected way, igniting a passion that would lead him to become one of the most influential figures in computer architecture. It was during his high school years when he first encountered a computer, a moment that would forever change the trajectory of his life.

The Initial Spark

In the early 1970s, as a teenager, Patterson was introduced to the world of computing through a rudimentary computer system, a DEC PDP-8, housed in a local community center. This machine, with its limited processing power and memory, was a far cry from the advanced systems of today, yet it held an allure that captivated Patterson. The PDP-8, often referred to as a "mini-computer," allowed him to explore the basics of programming through a simple language known as Assembly.

Learning the Basics

Patterson's first programming experience was not without its challenges. The Assembly language, while powerful, was notoriously difficult to master due to its low-level nature, requiring a deep understanding of the hardware. Each instruction had to be meticulously crafted, as the programmer was responsible for managing memory and registers directly. This hands-on experience with the machine's architecture laid the groundwork for Patterson's future innovations.

The syntax of Assembly language can be daunting for beginners, as it involves a series of mnemonics that correspond to machine-level instructions. For example, the instruction to load a value into a register might look like this:

```
LOAD R1, 0x00
```

This command would load the value stored at memory address 0x00 into register R1. Such low-level programming forced Patterson to think critically about how software interacts with hardware, a theme that would recur throughout his career.

The Joy of Problem-Solving

One of the most significant aspects of Patterson's early programming experiences was the thrill of problem-solving. He found immense satisfaction in debugging his code, a process that often involved painstakingly tracing through each line to identify errors. This process taught him the importance of precision and attention to detail, skills that would serve him well in his later research.

For instance, while working on a simple program to perform arithmetic operations, Patterson encountered a frustrating bug. His code would produce incorrect results for certain inputs. After hours of debugging, he discovered that he had overlooked a critical aspect of integer overflow, a common issue in programming. This experience not only honed his technical skills but also instilled a sense of resilience and determination.

The Influence of Mentorship

During this formative period, Patterson was fortunate to have mentors who recognized his potential. A particularly influential figure was his high school math teacher, Mr. Johnson, who encouraged him to explore the intricacies of programming beyond the basics. Mr. Johnson introduced Patterson to more advanced concepts, such as algorithms and data structures, which would become foundational elements in computer science.

The transition from Assembly to higher-level programming languages, such as FORTRAN and BASIC, opened new doors for Patterson. These languages abstracted many of the complexities of hardware interaction, allowing him to focus on solving problems rather than managing memory directly. This shift was crucial, as it enabled him to tackle more complex projects and explore the vast possibilities of software development.

A Vision for the Future

As Patterson's skills grew, so did his vision for what computers could achieve. He began to dream of a future where computers would not only assist in calculations but also revolutionize entire industries. This vision was influenced by the burgeoning field of computer science and the rapid advancements in technology during the 1970s.

Patterson's early experiences with programming instilled in him a belief that computers could be more than just machines; they could be powerful tools for creativity and innovation. This belief would drive him to pursue a career in technology, ultimately leading to his groundbreaking work in computer architecture.

Conclusion

David Patterson's first encounter with programming was a pivotal moment in his life. It was a journey filled with challenges, mentorship, and a growing passion for technology. The skills and insights he gained during this time laid the foundation for his future contributions to the field of computer science, particularly in the development of the Reduced Instruction Set Computer (RISC) architecture. This early experience not only shaped his career but also highlighted the transformative power of programming in shaping the future of technology.

The Influence of Science Fiction on Patterson's Dreams

David Patterson's journey into the world of computing was not solely a product of formal education or familial encouragement; it was significantly shaped by the imaginative realms of science fiction. From a young age, Patterson found himself captivated by the narratives of futuristic technologies and the possibilities they presented. This fascination laid the groundwork for his innovative thinking and problem-solving abilities, which would later manifest in his groundbreaking work on the RISC architecture.

Science fiction has long served as a fertile ground for inspiring technological advancements. Authors like Isaac Asimov, Arthur C. Clarke, and Philip K. Dick painted vivid pictures of advanced computing, artificial intelligence, and the ethical dilemmas that accompany technological progress. These narratives not only entertained young minds but also provoked critical thinking about the implications of technology on society. For Patterson, these stories ignited a spark of curiosity and ambition, urging him to explore the uncharted territories of computer science.

One notable example of science fiction's influence on Patterson occurred during his formative years when he read Asimov's *Foundation* series. The concept of psychohistory—a mathematical sociology that could predict the future of large populations—resonated deeply with Patterson. This idea of using data and algorithms to foresee trends and behaviors mirrored his later work in computer architecture, where he sought to optimize processing efficiency through innovative design principles.

Moreover, Patterson's engagement with science fiction was not limited to literature. The rise of science fiction films in the 1970s and 1980s, such as *Star Wars* and *Blade Runner*, further fueled his imagination. These cinematic masterpieces showcased advanced technologies, including robotics and artificial intelligence, which became the backbone of Patterson's aspirations. The visual representation of futuristic societies and their complex interactions with technology inspired him to envision a world where computing could revolutionize everyday life.

As Patterson delved deeper into his academic pursuits, he began to draw parallels between the speculative technologies depicted in science fiction and the realities of computer science. He recognized that many of the challenges faced in these narratives mirrored the obstacles he encountered in his research. For instance, the ethical dilemmas surrounding artificial intelligence, as portrayed in films like *2001: A Space Odyssey*, prompted Patterson to consider the moral implications of his work on computer architecture. He understood that as technology advanced, so too did the responsibility of technologists to ensure their creations served humanity positively.

Patterson's interest in science fiction also led him to explore the concept of the "Singularity," a term popularized by futurist Ray Kurzweil, which refers to a point in the future when technological growth becomes uncontrollable and irreversible, resulting in unforeseeable changes to human civilization. This notion resonated with Patterson as he contemplated the rapid evolution of computer architecture and its potential to reshape the world. He became increasingly aware of the need for sustainable and ethical technological development, a theme that frequently appears in science fiction narratives.

The influence of science fiction on Patterson's dreams is evident in his approach to innovation. He often emphasized the importance of creativity in problem-solving, a principle that aligns closely with the imaginative nature of science fiction. By encouraging his students and colleagues to think outside the box, Patterson fostered an environment where groundbreaking ideas could flourish. His vision for the future of computing was not just about improving existing technologies but about reimagining what was possible.

In conclusion, the influence of science fiction on David Patterson's dreams cannot be overstated. It provided him with a framework for understanding the potential of technology and its implications for society. The imaginative worlds crafted by science fiction writers served as both inspiration and cautionary tales, guiding Patterson in his quest to revolutionize computer architecture. As he navigated the complexities of the tech industry, the lessons learned from these narratives remained at the forefront of his mind, shaping his vision for a future where technology and humanity could coexist harmoniously.

$$\text{Innovative Thinking} = \text{Imagination} + \text{Critical Analysis} \tag{17}$$

This equation encapsulates Patterson's belief that the intersection of creativity and analytical thinking is essential for groundbreaking advancements in technology. By embracing the imaginative possibilities presented in science fiction, Patterson was able to push the boundaries of what was achievable in the realm of computing, ultimately leading to his pioneering work on the RISC architecture.

Exploring the Potential of Computer Science

Computer Science (CS) has emerged as a transformative discipline that fuels innovation across various sectors, from healthcare to entertainment, and even to the very fabric of our daily lives. As David Patterson embarked on his journey into the world of programming and computer architecture, he began to realize the vast potential that this field holds. This section explores the foundational concepts of computer science, the challenges it faces, and the revolutionary possibilities it offers.

The Foundations of Computer Science

At its core, computer science is the study of algorithms, data structures, and the principles of computation. It encompasses a variety of subfields, including:

- **Algorithms:** The step-by-step procedures for solving problems. For example, the QuickSort algorithm is a widely used method for sorting data efficiently. It operates with an average time complexity of $O(n \log n)$.

- **Data Structures:** The organization and storage formats that enable efficient access and modification of data. Common data structures include arrays, linked lists, trees, and graphs.

- **Computational Theory:** This area explores the fundamental limits of what can be computed. It includes concepts such as Turing machines and the Church-Turing thesis, which posits that any computation can be performed by a Turing machine.

The interplay between these foundational concepts allows computer scientists to design systems that are not only efficient but also scalable and robust.

Real-World Applications

The potential of computer science is vividly illustrated through its applications. Here are a few examples that highlight its impact:

- **Healthcare:** Machine learning algorithms are being used to analyze medical data and assist in diagnosing diseases. For instance, convolutional neural networks (CNNs) have shown remarkable success in image recognition tasks, such as identifying tumors in radiology images.

- **Finance:** Algorithmic trading systems leverage complex algorithms to execute trades at high speeds, capitalizing on minute price fluctuations. The efficiency of these systems can be modeled using the Black-Scholes equation, which helps in option pricing.

- **Transportation:** Autonomous vehicles rely on a combination of sensors, machine learning, and computer vision to navigate safely. The algorithms used in these systems must process vast amounts of data in real-time, presenting significant challenges in terms of reliability and safety.

Challenges in Computer Science

Despite its potential, the field of computer science faces several challenges:

- **Scalability:** As systems grow, maintaining performance becomes increasingly difficult. For example, the challenge of scaling databases is a critical issue for companies like Facebook and Google, which handle petabytes of data daily.

- **Security:** With the rise of cyber threats, ensuring the security of systems is paramount. The development of secure algorithms and protocols, such as RSA encryption, is essential to protect sensitive information.

- **Ethics:** The ethical implications of technology, including privacy concerns and algorithmic bias, are becoming increasingly important. Computer scientists must navigate these issues to ensure that technology serves the greater good.

Future Directions

Looking ahead, the potential of computer science continues to expand. Emerging fields such as quantum computing promise to revolutionize the way we process information. Quantum algorithms, such as Shor's algorithm, can factor large numbers exponentially faster than classical algorithms, which has profound implications for cryptography.

Additionally, the integration of artificial intelligence (AI) into various domains is set to redefine industries. AI's ability to learn from data and improve over time opens up possibilities for personalized experiences in areas like education, entertainment, and customer service.

Conclusion

In summary, the exploration of computer science reveals a landscape rich with opportunity and challenge. As David Patterson's journey unfolded, he tapped into this potential, pioneering advancements that would shape the future of computing. By embracing the principles of computer science, we can continue to innovate and address the pressing issues of our time, ensuring that technology remains a force for good in the world.

Excelling in Academic Studies

David Patterson's journey through academia was marked by a relentless pursuit of knowledge and a passion for computer science that set him apart from his peers. His academic achievements began to shine during his high school years, where his natural aptitude for mathematics and science became evident. This section explores Patterson's academic excellence, highlighting the key elements that contributed to his success.

Foundations of Academic Excellence

From an early age, Patterson exhibited a keen interest in mathematics, often finding himself captivated by the beauty of numbers and their applications. His high school teachers recognized his potential and encouraged him to explore advanced mathematics and science courses. This foundational knowledge would later serve as a springboard for his studies in computer science.

During his time at high school, Patterson excelled in subjects such as calculus and physics, which provided him with a solid understanding of the principles that underpin computer architecture. For instance, his grasp of calculus allowed him to comprehend complex algorithms, while his knowledge of physics gave him insights into the hardware aspects of computing.

Pursuing Higher Education

After graduating from high school, Patterson enrolled at the University of California, Berkeley, a decision that would prove pivotal in his academic career. Berkeley was renowned for its rigorous computer science program and its emphasis on research and innovation. Here, Patterson was exposed to leading scholars and groundbreaking research that would shape his understanding of computer architecture.

At Berkeley, Patterson's coursework included advanced algorithms, data structures, and computer organization. He quickly distinguished himself in these classes, often contributing to discussions and offering innovative solutions to complex problems. His professors noted his ability to think critically and approach challenges with a unique perspective.

Research Breakthroughs

Patterson's academic journey was not limited to coursework; he actively engaged in research projects that would lay the groundwork for his future contributions to computer architecture. Under the mentorship of prominent faculty members, he explored various topics, including instruction set design and performance optimization.

One of Patterson's significant research contributions during his time at Berkeley was the development of the RISC (Reduced Instruction Set Computer) architecture. This innovative approach to computer design emphasized a simplified instruction set, which allowed for faster execution of programs. The foundational equation that guided this architectural philosophy can be expressed as:

$$\text{Performance} = \frac{\text{Instructions}}{\text{Execution Time}} \tag{18}$$

By minimizing the number of instructions and optimizing their execution time, Patterson and his collaborators aimed to enhance overall system performance.

Collaboration and Innovation

Collaboration played a crucial role in Patterson's academic success. He formed study groups with fellow students, fostering an environment of shared learning and innovation. These collaborative efforts often led to the exchange of ideas and the development of new concepts that would later influence his research.

Patterson's ability to work effectively in teams was particularly evident during group projects, where he often took on leadership roles. His peers admired his ability to articulate complex ideas clearly and his willingness to help others understand challenging concepts. This collaborative spirit not only enriched his own learning experience but also contributed to the success of his peers.

Recognition and Awards

As Patterson continued to excel in his academic pursuits, he garnered recognition for his contributions to the field of computer science. He received several awards and scholarships, including the prestigious National Science Foundation Fellowship, which provided him with the opportunity to further his research.

Patterson's academic achievements were not limited to individual accolades; he also contributed to the university's reputation as a leader in computer science education. His work on RISC architecture gained attention from industry leaders, paving the way for future innovations and collaborations.

Conclusion

David Patterson's academic journey was characterized by excellence, collaboration, and a commitment to pushing the boundaries of computer science. His early experiences in high school, combined with his rigorous studies at Berkeley, laid the foundation for his groundbreaking contributions to computer architecture. As he continued to excel in his academic pursuits, Patterson's passion for technology and innovation became evident, setting the stage for his future endeavors in the tech world.

This section highlights the importance of a solid academic foundation, collaborative learning, and recognition in shaping a successful career in technology. Patterson's journey serves as an inspiration to aspiring technologists, emphasizing that excellence in academic studies is a crucial stepping stone toward achieving greatness in the field of computer science.

The Decision to Pursue a Career in Technology

David Patterson's journey toward a career in technology was not merely a series of academic decisions; it was a profound awakening to the limitless possibilities that the digital world offered. This pivotal moment, rooted in his formative years, was influenced by a blend of personal passion, environmental factors, and the burgeoning excitement surrounding the field of computer science.

The Catalyst of Curiosity

From an early age, Patterson displayed an insatiable curiosity about how things worked. His childhood was marked by a fascination with gadgets and machines, often dismantling household electronics to understand their inner workings. This propensity for exploration was further fueled by the advent of personal computers in the late 1970s and early 1980s, a period when technology began to permeate everyday life. The introduction of user-friendly programming languages, like BASIC, made programming more accessible and ignited Patterson's imagination.

$$\text{Curiosity} = f(\text{Exposure to Technology}, \text{Hands-on Experience}) \tag{19}$$

In this equation, curiosity is a function of exposure to technology and hands-on experience. Patterson's early interactions with computers allowed him to cultivate a deep understanding of their potential, laying the groundwork for his future endeavors.

Influence of Mentorship

Mentorship played a crucial role in Patterson's decision to pursue technology as a career. During his high school years, he encountered several influential teachers who recognized his aptitude for mathematics and science. They encouraged him to delve deeper into these subjects, guiding him toward advanced coursework that included computer science. One pivotal moment came when a particularly inspiring teacher introduced him to the concept of algorithms and data structures, which captivated Patterson's analytical mind.

$$\text{Career Decision} = \text{Passion} + \text{Mentorship} + \text{Opportunity} \tag{20}$$

This equation illustrates how Patterson's career decision was not solely based on passion but was significantly influenced by mentorship and the opportunities that arose during his academic journey.

Academic Pursuits and Revelations

As Patterson progressed through his academic career, he enrolled at the University of California, Berkeley, where he was immersed in a rigorous curriculum that challenged him intellectually. It was here that he encountered the groundbreaking research of his professors and the vibrant community of innovators that thrived within the university's walls. The collaborative environment encouraged Patterson to engage in research projects, pushing the boundaries of what was possible in computer architecture.

The realization that technology could solve real-world problems solidified Patterson's commitment to the field. He began to see programming not just as a skill but as a powerful tool for innovation. This epiphany was critical, as it aligned with his desire to make a meaningful impact on society.

The Birth of RISC Architecture

The decision to pursue a career in technology culminated in Patterson's groundbreaking work on Reduced Instruction Set Computer (RISC) architecture. This pivotal moment in his career was not merely about technical achievement; it represented a shift in how computers could be designed and utilized. The RISC philosophy emphasized simplicity and efficiency, which resonated with Patterson's vision of making computing accessible and powerful.

The equation representing this moment can be expressed as:

$$\text{RISC Impact} = \text{Simplicity} \times \text{Efficiency} \tag{21}$$

This equation highlights how the principles of simplicity and efficiency were multiplied to create a significant impact on the computing landscape, ultimately influencing countless technologies that followed.

Challenges and Resilience

Pursuing a career in technology was not without its challenges. Patterson faced skepticism from traditionalists who were resistant to the RISC approach, often defending his ideas against criticism from industry leaders. However, his resilience in the face of adversity only strengthened his resolve. He understood that innovation often requires challenging the status quo, and he was willing to take risks to achieve his vision.

$$\text{Resilience} = \frac{\text{Overcoming Challenges}}{\text{Skepticism}} \tag{22}$$

This equation illustrates how Patterson's resilience was a function of his ability to overcome challenges relative to the skepticism he faced.

Conclusion: A Visionary Path Forward

Ultimately, David Patterson's decision to pursue a career in technology was shaped by a confluence of factors: his early curiosity, the influence of mentors, academic rigor, and a commitment to innovation. His journey reflects the essence of what it means to be a visionary in the tech industry—embracing challenges, fostering collaboration, and relentlessly pursuing a passion that has the potential to change the world.

As he moved forward, Patterson not only embraced his role as a pioneer in computer architecture but also became an advocate for open-source technologies, ensuring that the future of computing would be inclusive and accessible to all. His legacy is a testament to the power of following one's passion and the impact that one individual can have on the entire computing landscape.

The Formation of Patterson's Core Values

David Patterson's journey through the world of computer science has not only been marked by groundbreaking innovations but also by the core values that he has cultivated throughout his life. These values have shaped his approach to technology, education, and collaboration, influencing not only his work but also the broader tech community. This section delves into the formation of Patterson's core values, examining their origins, implications, and the impact they have had on his career and the industry at large.

1. Passion for Learning

From an early age, Patterson exhibited an insatiable curiosity about the world around him. This passion for learning was nurtured by his family, who encouraged him to explore his interests in science and technology. In his formative years, Patterson often found himself immersed in books about computers and programming, leading to a lifelong commitment to education and knowledge acquisition.

$$L = \sum_{i=1}^{n} E_i \tag{23}$$

Where L represents learning, and E_i denotes individual experiences that contribute to knowledge. This equation illustrates that Patterson's learning is a cumulative process, shaped by various experiences, both academic and personal.

2. Advocacy for Open Source

Patterson's belief in the importance of open-source technology stems from his early encounters with the limitations of proprietary systems. He recognized that access to technology should not be restricted by financial or corporate barriers. This conviction led him to advocate for open-source solutions, which democratize access to technology and foster innovation.

In 2010, Patterson co-founded the RISC-V Foundation, promoting an open standard for instruction set architecture. This initiative embodies his belief that collaboration and transparency in technology can lead to greater advancements and inclusivity.

3. Commitment to Integrity

Integrity has been a guiding principle for Patterson throughout his career. He believes that ethical considerations should be at the forefront of technological advancements. This commitment is evident in his stance on data privacy and security, where he emphasizes the responsibility of technologists to protect user information.

Patterson's approach can be summarized by the following ethical framework:

$$E = \frac{C}{R} \tag{24}$$

Where E represents ethical behavior, C denotes commitment to values, and R reflects the responsibility held by technologists. A higher commitment to values leads to greater ethical behavior, emphasizing the importance of integrity in tech.

4. Collaboration and Community

Patterson has consistently emphasized the importance of collaboration in driving innovation. He believes that the best ideas often emerge from diverse teams working together towards common goals. This value is reflected in his collaborative research efforts, particularly during his time at UC Berkeley, where he worked closely with peers, including John L. Hennessy.

The equation for collaborative success can be expressed as:

$$S = \sum_{j=1}^{m} (T_j \cdot C_j) \tag{25}$$

Where S is the success of the collaboration, T_j represents the talent of each team member, and C_j denotes the level of collaboration. This equation highlights the synergistic effect of teamwork, which Patterson has championed throughout his career.

5. Inspiration and Mentorship

Patterson's journey has been profoundly influenced by the mentors who guided him along the way. He recognizes the importance of giving back to the community by inspiring and mentoring the next generation of technologists. This commitment is reflected in his involvement with educational initiatives and outreach programs aimed at underrepresented groups in technology.

He often states:

> "Success is not just about what you achieve, but also about how you inspire others to reach their potential."

This philosophy underscores the value he places on mentorship and the ripple effect of positive influence in the tech community.

Conclusion

The formation of David Patterson's core values—passion for learning, advocacy for open source, commitment to integrity, collaboration, and mentorship—have been instrumental in shaping his career and contributions to the computing industry. These values not only define who he is as a technologist but also serve as guiding principles for future generations. As the tech landscape continues to evolve, Patterson's commitment to these ideals remains a beacon for aspiring programmers and innovators seeking to make a meaningful impact in the world.

Section Two: Academic Journey and Research Breakthroughs

Enrolling at the University of California, Berkeley

In the early 1970s, a young David Patterson made a pivotal decision that would shape the future of computer architecture: he enrolled at the University of California, Berkeley. This choice was not merely a step toward higher education; it was the launching pad for a career that would revolutionize computing. Berkeley, renowned for its rigorous academic environment and innovative spirit, offered Patterson an ideal setting to cultivate his burgeoning interest in technology and programming.

The Allure of Berkeley

The University of California, Berkeley, was a hotbed of intellectual activity during this period. The campus buzzed with ideas, debates, and a palpable energy that attracted some of the brightest minds in science and engineering. For Patterson, Berkeley represented an opportunity to immerse himself in a culture of innovation. The university's emphasis on research and development aligned perfectly with his aspirations, providing him with access to cutting-edge technology and influential mentors.

A New World of Learning

Upon his arrival, Patterson was immediately captivated by the depth of knowledge that surrounded him. The Computer Science Division at Berkeley was at the forefront of the computing revolution, and Patterson quickly found his niche. He enrolled in courses that challenged his understanding of programming languages, algorithms, and computer architecture. Notably, he was introduced to the concept of *machine architecture*, which would later become a cornerstone of his research.

The curriculum was rigorous, and Patterson faced challenges that tested his resolve. One of the significant hurdles was understanding the complexities of *instruction sets* and how they influenced the performance of computer systems. An instruction set defines the operations a computer can perform, and Patterson's fascination with this topic would lead him to explore how simplifying these sets could enhance efficiency.

For example, in traditional Complex Instruction Set Computing (CISC) architectures, a single instruction could execute multiple operations. This complexity often resulted in slower processing times due to the overhead of decoding these instructions. Patterson began to theorize that a Reduced Instruction Set Computing (RISC) approach, which utilized a smaller set of simple instructions, could lead to faster execution and improved performance.

Mentorship and Collaboration

At Berkeley, Patterson was fortunate to work alongside pioneering figures in computer science. One of his most influential mentors was Professor John L. Hennessy, who would later become a key collaborator in the development of RISC architecture. Hennessy's insights into computer organization and design provided Patterson with a robust framework for his research.

Their collaboration was characterized by a shared vision: to redefine the way computers processed instructions. This partnership would eventually lead to groundbreaking research that challenged the status quo of computing. Together, they explored the implications of RISC architecture, conducting experiments that demonstrated its potential advantages over traditional architectures.

$$T_{RISC} = \frac{C \cdot I}{F} \tag{26}$$

Where:

- T_{RISC} = Execution time for RISC
- C = Number of clock cycles per instruction
- I = Number of instructions
- F = Clock frequency

This equation illustrated Patterson's hypothesis that by reducing the number of cycles needed to execute instructions (C), RISC could achieve faster processing times, thus revolutionizing how computer systems operated.

Research Breakthroughs

The environment at Berkeley was conducive to experimentation and innovation. Patterson and his peers conducted various projects that pushed the boundaries of existing knowledge. One notable project involved the development of a prototype RISC processor, which showcased the viability of their theoretical concepts. This prototype, built with simplicity in mind, was a stark contrast to the complex architectures dominating the market.

Patterson's work did not go unnoticed. His research papers began to attract attention, and he was invited to present his findings at conferences. These opportunities not only bolstered his confidence but also established him as a thought leader in the field. The recognition he received at this stage of his career laid the groundwork for future collaborations and advancements in computer architecture.

The Spirit of Innovation

Enrolling at the University of California, Berkeley, was more than an academic choice for David Patterson; it was a transformative experience that ignited his passion for computer science. The challenges he faced, the mentors who guided him, and the collaborative spirit of the university all contributed to his development as a pioneering researcher.

As Patterson delved deeper into the world of computer architecture, he became increasingly aware of the societal implications of his work. He recognized that the advancements in computing technology had the potential to change lives and reshape industries. This awareness fueled his commitment to making technology accessible and efficient, a theme that would resonate throughout his career.

In conclusion, Patterson's enrollment at Berkeley marked the beginning of a remarkable journey. The knowledge he gained, the relationships he built, and the challenges he overcame during this formative period laid the foundation for his future contributions to the field of computer architecture. It was here that the seeds of RISC were sown, setting the stage for a revolution in computing that would impact generations to come.

Mentors and Role Models at Berkeley

David Patterson's journey through the University of California, Berkeley, was not merely an academic pursuit; it was a transformative experience shaped by the guidance of influential mentors and role models. This section explores the profound impact these figures had on Patterson's development as a computer scientist and architect, highlighting their contributions to his pioneering work in Reduced Instruction Set Computing (RISC).

The Influence of Professors

At Berkeley, Patterson was surrounded by a cadre of esteemed professors who left an indelible mark on his academic and professional trajectory. Among them, Professor **John L. Hennessy** stood out as a pivotal figure. Hennessy, a visionary in the field of computer architecture, became a mentor and collaborator to Patterson. Their partnership blossomed as they explored the intricacies of processor design, leading to groundbreaking research on RISC.

Hennessy's approach to education emphasized not only theoretical understanding but also practical application. He often encouraged his students to engage in hands-on projects, fostering an environment where innovative ideas could flourish. This philosophy resonated with Patterson, who thrived in the dynamic academic atmosphere of Berkeley.

Research Collaboration and Innovation

The collaboration between Patterson and Hennessy culminated in the development of the RISC architecture. Their research focused on simplifying the instruction set of computer processors to enhance performance and efficiency. The core idea can be expressed mathematically as:

$$\text{Performance} \propto \frac{\text{Number of Instructions Executed}}{\text{Execution Time}} \tag{27}$$

This equation highlights the relationship between the number of instructions executed and the time taken for execution, a principle that underpinned their work on RISC. By reducing the complexity of instructions, Patterson and Hennessy were able to improve the overall performance of processors, setting the stage for a revolution in computer architecture.

Role Models Beyond Academia

In addition to Hennessy, Patterson drew inspiration from several other role models during his time at Berkeley. Notably, **David L. Parnas**, a pioneer in software engineering, influenced Patterson's thinking about modular design and the importance of clear specifications. Parnas's work on information hiding and modular programming introduced Patterson to the concept of designing systems that are robust and maintainable.

Patterson also found motivation in the achievements of **Barbara Liskov**, who was one of the first women to earn a Ph.D. in computer science. Liskov's contributions to programming languages and software design served as a powerful reminder of the diverse paths within the tech industry. Her work on the Liskov Substitution Principle (LSP) emphasized the importance of abstraction and polymorphism, concepts that would later inform Patterson's architectural designs.

Networking and Professional Development

Berkeley provided Patterson with a unique platform for networking with industry leaders and fellow researchers. Attending seminars and workshops allowed him to engage with prominent figures in computer science, including **Andrew S. Tanenbaum**, known for his work in operating systems and computer networks. These interactions not only expanded Patterson's knowledge base but also helped him build a professional network that would prove invaluable throughout his career.

The environment at Berkeley encouraged collaboration and knowledge sharing among students and faculty. Patterson often participated in study groups and research projects, fostering a sense of camaraderie and intellectual curiosity. This collaborative spirit was crucial in shaping his approach to problem-solving and innovation.

Conclusion: The Lasting Impact of Mentorship

The mentors and role models Patterson encountered during his time at Berkeley played a significant role in his development as a computer scientist. Their guidance, encouragement, and innovative ideas laid the groundwork for his future contributions to the field of computer architecture. The relationships he cultivated during this formative period not only influenced his academic pursuits but also instilled in him the values of collaboration, integrity, and a commitment to advancing technology for the greater good.

As Patterson embarked on his journey to revolutionize computer architecture with RISC, he carried the lessons learned from his mentors, demonstrating that the impact of mentorship extends far beyond the classroom. It is through the support and inspiration of those who came before him that Patterson was able to navigate the challenges of the tech industry and emerge as a leading figure in computer science.

Patterson's Groundbreaking Research on RISC

David Patterson's research on Reduced Instruction Set Computer (RISC) architecture in the 1980s marked a pivotal shift in computer design that has profoundly influenced the computing landscape. The core philosophy behind RISC is to simplify the instruction set of the processor, allowing for more efficient execution of instructions, which ultimately enhances performance. This section delves into Patterson's innovative research, highlighting the theoretical foundations, problems addressed, and examples that illustrate the impact of RISC.

Theoretical Foundations of RISC

The RISC architecture is predicated on the idea that a smaller set of instructions can lead to higher performance through various means, including pipelining, which allows multiple instruction phases to overlap. This contrasts sharply with Complex Instruction Set Computing (CISC), where processors are designed with a large number of instructions, many of which are rarely used. The RISC philosophy can be encapsulated in the following principles:

- **Simplicity of Instructions:** Each instruction should perform a simple operation, allowing for faster execution.

- **Load/Store Architecture:** Only load and store instructions can access memory, while all other instructions operate on registers, minimizing memory access delays.

- **Fixed Instruction Length:** Using a uniform instruction length simplifies instruction decoding and enhances pipelining efficiency.
- **Emphasis on Compiler Optimization:** A RISC design relies heavily on the compiler to optimize instruction scheduling and resource allocation.

Mathematically, the performance improvement can be expressed using the formula:

$$\text{Performance} = \frac{\text{Number of Instructions Executed} \times \text{Cycles Per Instruction}}{\text{Execution Time}} \tag{28}$$

By reducing the cycles per instruction through efficient pipelining and optimizing the number of instructions executed, RISC architectures can achieve superior performance.

Addressing Key Problems in Computer Architecture

Patterson's research sought to address several key problems that plagued existing architectures. One significant issue was the inefficiency of CISC architectures, which often included many rarely used instructions that complicated the design and increased the time taken to execute programs. By streamlining the instruction set, Patterson demonstrated that RISC could achieve higher performance with fewer transistors dedicated to instruction decoding.

Another problem was the challenge of achieving high clock speeds. The complexity of CISC instructions often resulted in longer execution times, making it difficult to increase clock speeds without sacrificing performance. In contrast, RISC's simplified instructions allowed for higher clock rates, as the processor could execute instructions more quickly.

Pioneering Research and Breakthroughs

Patterson, in collaboration with his colleague John L. Hennessy, conducted pioneering research that led to the development of the RISC architecture. Their work culminated in the design of the RISC I processor at the University of California, Berkeley, which was one of the first implementations of RISC principles. The RISC I processor featured a simple instruction set, with 32 instructions, all of which were designed to execute in a single clock cycle.

The RISC I architecture was further refined with the development of the RISC II processor, which introduced enhancements such as a larger register file and support for pipelined execution. This evolution demonstrated the practicality and effectiveness of the RISC design, leading to increased interest from both academia and industry.

Real-World Applications and Impact

The impact of Patterson's research on RISC architecture can be seen in numerous modern processors, including those used in smartphones, tablets, and servers. Companies such as ARM and MIPS have adopted RISC principles, leading to widespread adoption of RISC-based designs in mobile and embedded systems.

For example, ARM processors, which are based on RISC architecture, have become the dominant architecture in mobile computing, powering billions of devices worldwide. The efficiency of RISC has allowed ARM processors to deliver high performance while maintaining low power consumption, a crucial factor for battery-operated devices.

Moreover, the introduction of RISC-V, an open standard instruction set architecture (ISA) based on RISC principles, has further solidified Patterson's legacy. RISC-V allows researchers and companies to innovate freely, fostering a new wave of processor design that adheres to the RISC philosophy.

Conclusion

David Patterson's groundbreaking research on RISC architecture has left an indelible mark on the field of computer science. By advocating for a simplified instruction set, Patterson not only addressed key challenges in computer architecture but also laid the groundwork for future innovations. The principles of RISC continue to influence modern processor design, showcasing the enduring relevance of Patterson's work in shaping the future of computing.

The Evolution of Computer Architecture

The evolution of computer architecture is a fascinating journey that reflects the relentless pursuit of efficiency, performance, and adaptability in computing systems. From the early days of simple mechanical calculators to the complex multi-core processors of today, each phase of development has been marked by significant breakthroughs and paradigm shifts.

Early Beginnings: The Mechanical Era

The story begins in the 19th century with pioneers like Charles Babbage, who conceptualized the Analytical Engine, an early mechanical general-purpose computer. Although never completed, Babbage's design introduced fundamental concepts such as conditional branching and loops, which would later become cornerstones of modern programming.

The Vacuum Tube Revolution

The advent of vacuum tubes in the early 20th century marked a significant leap in computational power. The Electronic Numerical Integrator and Computer (ENIAC), completed in 1945, was one of the first electronic general-purpose computers. It utilized approximately 18,000 vacuum tubes, allowing it to perform calculations much faster than its mechanical predecessors. However, the use of vacuum tubes also posed challenges, including heat generation and reliability issues.

Transistors: A Game Changer

The invention of the transistor in 1947 revolutionized computer architecture by providing a more reliable and energy-efficient alternative to vacuum tubes. Transistors enabled the development of smaller, faster, and more affordable computers. The introduction of the IBM 1401 in 1959 showcased the potential of transistor-based systems, leading to widespread adoption in businesses and academia.

The Birth of Microprocessors

The 1970s witnessed the emergence of microprocessors, which integrated the functions of a computer's central processing unit (CPU) onto a single chip. The Intel 4004, released in 1971, was the first commercially available microprocessor, paving the way for personal computing. This era saw the democratization of computing, as individuals gained access to machines that were once the domain of large corporations.

The Rise of RISC and CISC Architectures

As computer systems evolved, so too did the architectures that governed their design. The two dominant philosophies emerged: Reduced Instruction Set

Computer (RISC) and Complex Instruction Set Computer (CISC). RISC architectures, championed by David Patterson and John L. Hennessy, emphasized a smaller set of simple instructions that could be executed in a single clock cycle. This approach led to increased performance and efficiency, particularly in applications requiring high-speed processing.

In contrast, CISC architectures, exemplified by the x86 family of processors, aimed to provide a rich set of complex instructions that could perform multiple tasks in a single operation. While CISC systems offered versatility, they often suffered from slower execution times due to the complexity of decoding and executing instructions.

The Shift Towards Parallelism

The late 20th century ushered in a new era characterized by the need for parallelism. As applications became more demanding, computer architects sought ways to enhance performance through multi-core and multi-threaded designs. The introduction of multi-core processors allowed for simultaneous execution of multiple threads, significantly improving computational efficiency. For example, Intel's Core i7 processor, launched in 2008, featured four cores capable of executing eight threads simultaneously, showcasing the power of parallel processing.

Emergence of GPUs and Accelerators

As the demand for high-performance computing surged, Graphics Processing Units (GPUs) emerged as powerful accelerators for parallel processing tasks. Initially designed for rendering graphics, GPUs proved exceptionally well-suited for data-intensive applications such as machine learning and scientific simulations. The rise of frameworks like CUDA and OpenCL enabled developers to harness the parallel processing capabilities of GPUs, leading to breakthroughs in fields ranging from artificial intelligence to computational biology.

The Era of Heterogeneous Computing

In recent years, the concept of heterogeneous computing has gained traction, where systems leverage multiple types of processors to optimize performance for specific workloads. This approach allows for a more efficient allocation of resources, as different processors excel at different tasks. For instance, a system might utilize a CPU for general-purpose tasks while offloading compute-intensive operations to a GPU or a specialized accelerator.

Future Directions: Quantum and Neuromorphic Computing

Looking ahead, the evolution of computer architecture is poised to take new directions with the advent of quantum computing and neuromorphic computing. Quantum computers leverage the principles of quantum mechanics to perform calculations at unprecedented speeds, offering the potential to solve problems that are currently intractable for classical computers. On the other hand, neuromorphic computing seeks to emulate the structure and function of the human brain, enabling more efficient processing of complex data patterns.

Conclusion

The evolution of computer architecture is a testament to human ingenuity and the relentless quest for progress. Each phase of development has brought forth new challenges and opportunities, shaping the way we interact with technology. As we stand on the brink of new frontiers, the future of computer architecture promises to be as dynamic and transformative as its storied past.

Collaborating with John L. Hennessy

In the realm of computer architecture, few partnerships have been as impactful as that of David Patterson and John L. Hennessy. Their collaboration not only shaped the future of RISC (Reduced Instruction Set Computer) architecture but also set a precedent for how academic research could influence industry practices. This section delves into the dynamics of their partnership, the challenges they faced, and the groundbreaking outcomes that emerged from their joint efforts.

The Genesis of Collaboration

David Patterson and John L. Hennessy first crossed paths at the University of California, Berkeley, where they were both faculty members. Their shared interests in computer architecture and the quest for more efficient processing led them to engage in discussions that would eventually evolve into a collaborative research effort. Hennessy, who had already established a reputation for his work on computer architecture, brought a complementary skill set to the partnership. Together, they aimed to explore the limitations of traditional CISC (Complex Instruction Set Computer) architectures and to advocate for a more streamlined approach.

Theoretical Foundations of RISC

At the heart of their collaboration was the RISC philosophy, which emphasized a simplified instruction set that could be executed in a single clock cycle. This was a departure from the CISC approach, which relied on a more complex set of instructions that often required multiple cycles to execute. The RISC design philosophy can be encapsulated in the following equation:

$$\text{Performance} = \frac{\text{Instructions}}{\text{Cycles} \times \text{Cycle Time}} \tag{29}$$

By reducing the number of cycles per instruction and minimizing the cycle time through architectural simplifications, Patterson and Hennessy demonstrated that RISC could significantly enhance processing speed and efficiency.

Challenges in Implementation

Despite the theoretical advantages of RISC, Patterson and Hennessy faced substantial challenges in persuading the computing community to adopt this new paradigm. Established companies and researchers were deeply entrenched in CISC architectures, and there was considerable skepticism regarding the practicality of RISC. The duo encountered resistance from industry leaders who were reluctant to abandon their existing investments in CISC technologies.

To address these challenges, Patterson and Hennessy conducted extensive empirical research, demonstrating the performance benefits of RISC through a series of benchmarks. They published their findings in influential papers and presented them at conferences, gradually winning over skeptics in the academic and industrial sectors.

Key Contributions and Innovations

One of the most significant outcomes of their collaboration was the development of the RISC I processor, which was a proof-of-concept implementation of the RISC architecture. The RISC I project showcased the potential for higher performance through a simplified instruction set and became a cornerstone of their research.

In addition to the RISC I processor, Patterson and Hennessy co-authored the seminal textbook, *Computer Organization and Design: The Hardware/Software Interface*, which has become a foundational text in computer architecture courses worldwide. This textbook not only solidified their contributions to the field but also educated countless students and professionals on the principles of RISC architecture.

The Legacy of Their Partnership

The collaboration between Patterson and Hennessy transcended their individual achievements, leading to the establishment of a robust academic and research community focused on RISC architecture. Their work inspired a new generation of computer scientists and engineers to explore innovative approaches to processor design.

Furthermore, their partnership laid the groundwork for the RISC-V initiative, which aims to create an open standard for RISC architecture. This initiative reflects their ongoing commitment to advancing computer architecture in a way that is accessible and beneficial to a wide array of industries.

In conclusion, the collaboration between David Patterson and John L. Hennessy stands as a testament to the power of partnership in academia. Through their combined efforts, they not only revolutionized computer architecture but also fostered a culture of innovation that continues to influence the field today. Their legacy is a reminder that collaboration can lead to breakthroughs that change the landscape of technology forever.

The Birth of the RISC Processor

In the early 1980s, a revolutionary concept began to take shape at the University of California, Berkeley, led by David Patterson and his team. This concept was the Reduced Instruction Set Computer (RISC) architecture, which aimed to simplify the design of computer processors by reducing the complexity of instructions that the hardware needed to execute. The birth of the RISC processor marked a significant shift in computer architecture and set the stage for modern computing.

Theoretical Foundations

The theoretical underpinnings of RISC architecture were rooted in the observation that most programs tend to use a small subset of instructions frequently, while others are rarely employed. This insight was encapsulated in the principle of *locality of reference,* which suggests that optimizing for the most commonly used instructions could yield significant performance gains. The RISC philosophy posits that by minimizing the number of instructions, a processor can execute instructions more efficiently, leading to higher performance.

The RISC design philosophy is characterized by several key principles:

- **Simplicity of Instruction Set:** RISC architectures utilize a smaller number of simple instructions that can be executed in a single clock cycle. This contrasts with Complex Instruction Set Computers (CISC), which have a larger number of more complex instructions.

- **Load/Store Architecture:** RISC architectures separate memory access from computation, meaning that operations are performed on registers rather than directly on memory. This reduces the number of cycles needed for memory access.

- **Register-Based Operations:** RISC processors typically have a larger number of general-purpose registers, allowing for more efficient data handling and reducing the need for frequent memory access.

- **Pipelining:** The RISC architecture is designed to take advantage of pipelining, a technique that allows multiple instruction phases to overlap, thereby increasing instruction throughput.

Design Challenges and Solutions

The journey to the RISC processor was not without its challenges. One of the primary hurdles was the skepticism from the existing computing community, which was heavily invested in CISC architectures. Critics argued that simplifying the instruction set would lead to a loss of functionality and performance. However, Patterson and his team were undeterred.

To demonstrate the viability of RISC, Patterson's group embarked on a series of experiments to compare the performance of RISC and CISC architectures. They developed a prototype processor called the *RISC I*, which was designed to implement the core principles of RISC.

The design of RISC I included the following features:

- A simple instruction set with 32 instructions, each designed to execute in a single cycle.

- A register file with 32 general-purpose registers, enabling efficient data manipulation.

- A load/store architecture that separated data transfer from computation.

The results from these experiments were promising. RISC I demonstrated that it could execute instructions at a much faster rate compared to its CISC counterparts, validating the RISC design principles.

The RISC II and Beyond

Building on the success of RISC I, Patterson and his team developed the RISC II processor. RISC II incorporated enhancements based on the lessons learned from RISC I and introduced features such as:

- Improved pipelining techniques, allowing for better instruction throughput.
- Support for more complex addressing modes while still adhering to the RISC philosophy.
- Enhanced performance metrics that showcased the practical benefits of RISC architecture.

The introduction of RISC II solidified the RISC architecture's position in the computing landscape. It became evident that the RISC approach was not just a theoretical exercise but a practical solution to the growing demands of computing performance.

Industry Adoption and Impact

As the RISC architecture gained traction, it attracted the attention of major technology companies. Industry giants began to recognize the potential of RISC for their products. Companies such as Sun Microsystems and MIPS Computer Systems began to develop RISC-based processors, leading to a proliferation of RISC architectures across various computing platforms.

The impact of RISC architecture was profound. It not only influenced the design of future processors but also sparked a broader movement towards open architectures and standardized instruction sets. The RISC principles laid the groundwork for the development of subsequent architectures, including ARM and RISC-V, which continue to dominate the market today.

Conclusion

The birth of the RISC processor marked a pivotal moment in the history of computing. David Patterson's vision and determination to challenge the status quo led to the creation of an architecture that fundamentally changed how processors were designed and utilized. The RISC philosophy emphasized simplicity, efficiency, and performance, principles that continue to resonate in the world of computer architecture. As we look to the future, the legacy of the RISC processor remains a testament to the power of innovation and the importance of questioning established norms in the pursuit of progress.

Challenges and Opposition in the Industry

David Patterson's groundbreaking work on Reduced Instruction Set Computing (RISC) was not without its fair share of challenges and opposition from within the tech industry. As Patterson and his collaborators sought to redefine computer architecture, they encountered a landscape rife with resistance, skepticism, and vested interests. This section delves into the multifaceted challenges Patterson faced, illustrating the complexities of innovation in a field often dominated by established norms and powerful entities.

The Established Paradigm: CISC Dominance

At the time Patterson was developing the RISC architecture, Complex Instruction Set Computing (CISC) was the prevailing paradigm. CISC architectures, characterized by their rich set of instructions, were deeply entrenched in the industry, with major players like Intel and IBM leading the charge. The dominance of CISC systems was not merely a matter of technical preference; it was also a reflection of substantial financial investments and a vast ecosystem of software tailored to these architectures. The entrenched interests of these companies posed a significant barrier to the acceptance of RISC.

One of the primary arguments against RISC was its perceived inefficiency in handling complex instructions. Critics claimed that the reduced instruction set would lead to increased code size and potentially slower performance for certain applications. This skepticism was encapsulated in the phrase "RISC is just a fad," which echoed throughout the industry. Patterson and his team had to not only develop a compelling technical framework but also persuade an entire industry to rethink its foundational beliefs about what constituted efficient computing.

The Technical Challenges of RISC

While the theoretical advantages of RISC were compelling—such as simplified instruction decoding and increased pipeline efficiency—implementing these concepts in practice was fraught with challenges. One significant technical hurdle was the need for compilers capable of optimizing code for RISC architectures. Early compilers were not well-equipped to handle the nuances of RISC, which required a different approach to instruction scheduling and resource allocation.

The equation governing the performance improvement of RISC over CISC can be expressed as:

$$\text{Performance} = \frac{\text{Instructions Executed} \times \text{Cycles per Instruction}}{\text{Execution Time}} \tag{30}$$

In this equation, the challenge lay in minimizing the cycles per instruction while managing the increase in the number of instructions executed due to the simpler instruction set. Patterson's team had to innovate not only in hardware design but also in software development to ensure that RISC could deliver on its promise.

Industry Pushback: The Political Landscape

The resistance Patterson faced was not limited to technical challenges; it also had a political dimension. The introduction of RISC architecture threatened the business models of established companies that had invested heavily in CISC technologies. These companies were not only concerned about losing market share but also about the potential obsolescence of their existing products and services.

Patterson's advocacy for RISC was met with pushback from industry leaders who viewed the new architecture as a threat to their established dominance. This opposition manifested in various forms, from public skepticism to lobbying against the adoption of RISC technologies in academic and commercial settings. Patterson's collaboration with John L. Hennessy, which ultimately led to the development of the MIPS architecture, was particularly contentious, as it directly challenged the status quo.

The Role of Academia and Research Funding

In addition to industry opposition, Patterson faced challenges within the academic community. The funding landscape for research in computer architecture was heavily influenced by industry preferences, which favored CISC architectures. Securing grants and resources for RISC-related research proved to be a daunting task, as many funding bodies were hesitant to support what they perceived as a radical departure from established norms.

Patterson's ability to navigate this challenging landscape was crucial. He leveraged his position at the University of California, Berkeley, to foster a collaborative environment that attracted like-minded researchers and students who were eager to explore the potential of RISC. This academic support network became vital in countering the industry's resistance, as it provided a platform for rigorous research and experimentation.

The Turning Point: Demonstrating RISC's Viability

Despite the numerous challenges, Patterson and his team persevered, focusing on demonstrating the practical viability of RISC through real-world applications. One of the pivotal moments in the acceptance of RISC came with the introduction of the SPARC architecture in the late 1980s, which showcased the potential of RISC in commercial systems. The success of SPARC was instrumental in shifting perceptions within the industry, as it provided a tangible example of RISC's advantages in terms of performance and efficiency.

Moreover, the emergence of the RISC-based ARM architecture further solidified the relevance of Patterson's work. ARM's adoption in mobile devices and embedded systems illustrated the scalability and versatility of RISC principles, ultimately leading to its dominance in these markets. This success story became a powerful counter-narrative to the skepticism that had initially surrounded RISC, demonstrating that innovation could indeed thrive in the face of opposition.

Conclusion: A Legacy of Resilience

The journey of David Patterson and the RISC architecture is a testament to the resilience required to challenge established norms in the tech industry. The opposition Patterson faced—from entrenched CISC advocates to funding challenges and industry pushback—was formidable. Yet, through a combination of technical innovation, academic collaboration, and strategic advocacy, Patterson was able to carve out a space for RISC in the computing landscape.

This section highlights not only the obstacles faced by Patterson but also the broader implications for innovation within the tech industry. It serves as a reminder that true progress often requires navigating a complex web of challenges, and that the courage to pursue one's vision can ultimately lead to transformative change.

The Impact of RISC on the Computing Landscape

The Reduced Instruction Set Computer (RISC) architecture has dramatically transformed the computing landscape since its inception in the 1980s. By simplifying the instruction set, RISC has enabled higher performance, greater efficiency, and a paradigm shift in how processors are designed and utilized. This section explores the multifaceted impact of RISC on computing, from its foundational principles to its influence on modern computing systems.

Foundational Principles of RISC

RISC architecture is characterized by a small, highly optimized instruction set that allows for more efficient execution. The fundamental principles of RISC include:

- **Simplicity:** RISC processors utilize a limited number of instructions, which can be executed in a single clock cycle. This simplicity reduces the complexity of the control unit and enhances performance.
- **Load/Store Architecture:** RISC employs a load/store architecture, where only load and store instructions access memory. This design allows for faster execution as it minimizes memory access times.
- **Pipelining:** RISC architectures are designed to take advantage of instruction pipelining, where multiple instruction phases (fetch, decode, execute) are overlapped. This significantly increases instruction throughput and overall performance.
- **Register-Based Operations:** RISC architectures make extensive use of registers, allowing for faster data access and manipulation compared to memory-based operations.

These principles have led to a significant performance boost in computing systems, making RISC a preferred choice for many applications.

Performance Improvements

The performance improvements brought about by RISC architecture can be quantified through various metrics. The execution time of a program can be expressed as:

$$\text{Execution Time} = \frac{\text{Number of Instructions}}{\text{Instructions per Cycle}} \times \text{Cycle Time} \tag{31}$$

Where: - **Number of Instructions** refers to the total number of instructions in a program. - **Instructions per Cycle** (IPC) indicates how many instructions are executed in one clock cycle, which is significantly higher in RISC architectures due to pipelining. - **Cycle Time** is the duration of a single clock cycle, which tends to be shorter in RISC due to simpler control logic.

By optimizing IPC through pipelining and reducing cycle time, RISC processors can achieve lower execution times compared to their Complex Instruction Set Computer (CISC) counterparts.

Influence on Modern Computing Systems

RISC architecture has not only influenced the design of individual processors but has also played a pivotal role in shaping modern computing systems. Its impact can be seen in several key areas:

- **Mobile Computing:** The advent of mobile devices has seen a significant shift towards RISC-based processors, such as ARM architecture. ARM processors are ubiquitous in smartphones and tablets, providing a balance of performance and power efficiency essential for mobile applications.

- **Embedded Systems:** RISC architectures dominate embedded systems due to their efficiency and low power consumption. From automotive controls to smart appliances, RISC-based processors are integral to the functionality of modern devices.

- **Cloud Computing and Data Centers:** RISC architectures have also made inroads into cloud computing and data centers. Companies like Amazon and Google have begun utilizing RISC-based chips for their servers, benefiting from the performance and energy efficiency that RISC offers.

The widespread adoption of RISC architectures across various domains illustrates its profound influence on the computing landscape.

Challenges and Limitations

Despite its advantages, RISC architecture is not without challenges. The transition from CISC to RISC has presented several hurdles:

- **Software Compatibility:** Legacy software designed for CISC architectures may require significant modification to run on RISC systems. This compatibility issue can hinder the adoption of RISC in certain environments.

- **Complexity of Compiler Design:** RISC architectures require sophisticated compiler designs to optimize code effectively. The need for advanced optimization techniques can complicate the development process.

- **Market Competition:** The dominance of CISC architectures, particularly x86, presents a significant barrier to the widespread adoption of RISC in personal computing and enterprise environments.

Case Studies: RISC in Action

To illustrate the impact of RISC on the computing landscape, we can examine a few notable case studies:

- **ARM Holdings:** ARM architecture has revolutionized the mobile computing industry. With its low power consumption and high performance, ARM processors have become the standard for smartphones, tablets, and IoT devices. The rise of ARM has led to a proliferation of mobile applications and services.
- **RISC-V:** The emergence of RISC-V as an open-source RISC architecture has sparked innovation in processor design. RISC-V allows researchers and developers to create customized processors for specific applications, fostering a new wave of innovation in computing.
- **IBM Power Architecture:** IBM's Power architecture, based on RISC principles, has been instrumental in high-performance computing. Power processors are widely used in data centers and supercomputing environments, showcasing the scalability and performance benefits of RISC.

These case studies highlight the versatility and impact of RISC architecture across different sectors of the computing landscape.

Conclusion

In conclusion, the impact of RISC on the computing landscape is profound and multifaceted. By simplifying instruction sets and optimizing performance, RISC architecture has paved the way for advancements in mobile computing, embedded systems, and high-performance computing. Despite facing challenges, RISC continues to influence the design and functionality of modern processors, ensuring its relevance in the ever-evolving world of technology. As we look to the future, the principles of RISC will undoubtedly continue to shape the next generation of computing innovations.

Recognition and Awards for Patterson's Work

David Patterson's contributions to computer architecture and the broader field of computer science have not gone unnoticed. Over his illustrious career, he has received numerous accolades and awards that underscore his impact and innovation in technology. This section delves into the significant recognitions that have marked Patterson's journey, reflecting both his pioneering work in Reduced Instruction Set Computing (RISC) and his commitment to advancing the field.

Key Awards and Honors

Patterson's work has been recognized by various prestigious organizations and institutions. Among the most notable awards are:

- **IEEE Medal of Honor (2010)**: This is one of the highest honors awarded by the Institute of Electrical and Electronics Engineers (IEEE). Patterson received this award for his contributions to the field of computer architecture, particularly for his role in the development of RISC architecture which significantly influenced modern computing.
- **ACM Turing Award (2017)**: Often referred to as the "Nobel Prize of Computing," the Turing Award was jointly awarded to Patterson and his collaborator John L. Hennessy for their pioneering work on RISC architecture. The citation highlighted their significant influence on the design of modern microprocessors and computer systems.
- **National Medal of Technology and Innovation (2018)**: Awarded by the President of the United States, this medal recognized Patterson's contributions to the field of technology and innovation, emphasizing his role in advancing computer architecture and education.
- **Member of the National Academy of Engineering (2000)**: Patterson was elected to this esteemed body in recognition of his contributions to engineering and technology, marking him as a leader in the field.

Impact of Awards on the Tech Community

The recognition of Patterson's work has had a profound effect on the tech community. His accolades serve as a beacon for aspiring engineers and computer scientists, illustrating the potential for innovation and excellence in the field. By receiving such prestigious awards, Patterson has not only validated his own work but also inspired a new generation of technologists to push the boundaries of what is possible in computer science.

Prominent Lectures and Keynotes

In addition to formal awards, Patterson has been invited to deliver keynote addresses at numerous conferences and symposiums worldwide. His talks often focus on the evolution of computing, the importance of open-source architecture, and the future of technology. Notable lectures include:

- **Keynote at the International Symposium on Computer Architecture (ISCA):** Patterson has been a recurring keynote speaker at ISCA, where he discusses the latest trends in computer architecture and the implications of RISC on future designs.

- **Distinguished Lecture Series at Various Universities:** Patterson has shared his insights at institutions such as MIT, Stanford, and UC Berkeley, emphasizing the importance of mentorship and education in the field of technology.

Publications and Citations

Patterson's influence is also evident in his extensive body of published work. His textbooks, particularly "Computer Organization and Design" co-authored with John L. Hennessy, have become essential resources in computer science education. The book has been cited extensively, showcasing its impact on both students and professionals in the field.

$$\text{Citations} = \sum_{i=1}^{n} \text{Citations of each work}_i \tag{32}$$

Where n is the total number of publications authored by Patterson. His research papers on RISC architecture are frequently referenced in academic literature, further solidifying his status as a leading figure in computer science.

Recognition Beyond Awards

Beyond formal awards, Patterson's work has been recognized in various forms of media and popular culture. His contributions have been featured in documentaries about the history of computing, and he has appeared in interviews discussing the future of technology. This visibility has helped to demystify complex topics in computer science for the general public, making them more accessible and engaging.

Conclusion

In conclusion, the recognition and awards bestowed upon David Patterson are a testament to his pioneering work in computer architecture and his lasting impact on the field. His accolades not only celebrate his achievements but also serve to inspire future generations of engineers and computer scientists to innovate and explore the boundaries of technology. As Patterson continues to contribute to the field, his legacy will undoubtedly influence the trajectory of computing for years to come.

The Legacy of RISC Architecture

The legacy of Reduced Instruction Set Computer (RISC) architecture is profound, reshaping the landscape of computing and influencing generations of computer scientists and engineers. RISC architecture emerged in the 1980s as a revolutionary approach to processor design, emphasizing simplicity and efficiency. This section delves into the key aspects of RISC's legacy, including its theoretical underpinnings, practical implications, and lasting impact on modern computing.

Theoretical Foundations

At its core, RISC architecture is grounded in the principle of simplifying the instruction set of a computer. The goal is to execute instructions in a single clock cycle, thus maximizing the performance of the processor. This approach contrasts sharply with Complex Instruction Set Computing (CISC), which incorporates a larger set of instructions that can perform multi-step operations within a single instruction. The foundational theory behind RISC can be summarized by the following equation:

$$\text{Performance} = \text{Instructions Per Cycle (IPC)} \times \text{Clock Rate} \tag{33}$$

Where: - Performance is the overall throughput of the processor. - IPC is maximized in RISC due to its streamlined instruction set. - Clock Rate is the speed at which the processor executes instructions.

By focusing on a reduced set of instructions, RISC architectures can achieve higher IPC, leading to improved performance. This theoretical framework laid the groundwork for subsequent developments in computer architecture.

Practical Implications

The practical implications of RISC architecture have been monumental. RISC processors, such as the MIPS, SPARC, and ARM, have become the backbone of many computing systems, from embedded devices to high-performance servers. One of the key advantages of RISC is its ability to optimize compiler design. With a simpler instruction set, compilers can generate more efficient machine code, which is crucial for performance.

For example, the ARM architecture, which is based on RISC principles, has become the dominant architecture in mobile devices. Its efficiency and power-saving capabilities have enabled the proliferation of smartphones and tablets. The ARM Cortex series exemplifies how RISC can lead to processors that provide high performance while consuming minimal power, making them ideal for battery-operated devices.

Challenges and Criticisms

Despite its successes, RISC architecture has faced challenges and criticisms. One significant issue is the increased complexity of software development. While RISC simplifies hardware design, it often requires more sophisticated compiler technology to fully exploit its capabilities. This can lead to longer development times and increased costs for software developers.

Furthermore, as applications have become more complex, the limitations of RISC have become apparent. Certain tasks that benefit from complex instructions may require additional programming effort, which can offset the advantages of simpler hardware. This ongoing debate between RISC and CISC continues to shape the evolution of computer architecture.

Legacy in Modern Computing

The legacy of RISC architecture is evident in the modern computing landscape. RISC principles have influenced the design of contemporary processors, including those used in personal computers, servers, and cloud computing infrastructures. The adoption of RISC principles in the design of graphics processing units (GPUs) and digital signal processors (DSPs) further showcases its versatility.

Moreover, the introduction of RISC-V, an open standard instruction set architecture, represents a significant evolution in RISC's legacy. RISC-V allows for customization and innovation while maintaining the core principles of RISC. Its open-source nature has garnered widespread interest in academia and industry, paving the way for new research and development opportunities.

Conclusion

In conclusion, the legacy of RISC architecture is a testament to the power of simplicity in computer design. Its theoretical foundations have influenced generations of computer scientists, while its practical implications have transformed the computing industry. Despite facing challenges and criticisms, RISC remains a cornerstone of modern computing, inspiring new innovations and shaping the future of technology. As we look ahead, the principles of RISC will undoubtedly continue to guide the evolution of computer architecture, ensuring its relevance for years to come.

Section Three: Unleashing a Revolutionary Approach

Introduction to the RISC Philosophy

The Reduced Instruction Set Computer (RISC) philosophy revolutionized computer architecture by emphasizing a streamlined set of instructions that can be executed efficiently. At its core, RISC aims to simplify the instruction set, allowing for faster execution of programs and improved performance in various computing tasks. This section will delve into the foundational principles of RISC, explore its theoretical underpinnings, discuss the problems it addresses, and provide examples that illustrate its impact on modern computing.

Theoretical Foundations of RISC

RISC architecture is built on several key theoretical principles:

- **Simplicity of Instruction Set:** RISC architectures utilize a small number of simple instructions. This simplicity allows for easier decoding and execution, as each instruction can be executed in a single clock cycle. The fundamental idea is that a limited instruction set can lead to higher performance, as seen in the equation:

$$\text{Performance} = \frac{\text{Number of Instructions}}{\text{Execution Time}}$$

- **Load/Store Architecture:** RISC architectures separate memory access from computation, using load and store instructions to move data between registers and memory. This design reduces complexity and enhances speed, as operations are performed on data stored in registers rather than directly in memory.

- **Pipeline Processing:** RISC designs are optimized for pipelining, where multiple instruction phases are overlapped. This allows for increased throughput, as different stages of instruction execution can occur simultaneously. A typical RISC pipeline might consist of five stages: Fetch, Decode, Execute, Memory Access, and Write Back.
- **Register-Based Operations:** RISC architectures rely heavily on registers for operations, minimizing the need for slow memory access. This is encapsulated in the formula:

  $$\text{Execution Time} \propto \text{Memory Access Time} \times \text{Number of Memory Accesses}$$

  By reducing memory accesses, RISC architectures can significantly enhance performance.

Addressing Problems in Computing

The RISC philosophy addresses several key problems faced by traditional Complex Instruction Set Computers (CISC):

- **Complexity in Instruction Decoding:** CISC architectures often feature a wide array of complex instructions, making decoding and execution more challenging. RISC's simplified instruction set allows for faster decoding and execution, reducing the overall complexity of the CPU design.
- **Execution Speed:** By focusing on executing instructions in a single clock cycle, RISC architectures can achieve higher performance levels. This is particularly important in high-performance computing environments where speed is critical.
- **Energy Efficiency:** The RISC philosophy promotes energy-efficient designs, as simpler instructions require less power to execute. This is especially relevant in mobile and embedded systems, where battery life is paramount.

Real-World Examples of RISC Implementation

Several notable examples of RISC architectures highlight the effectiveness of this philosophy:

- **ARM Architecture:** The ARM architecture is one of the most widely used RISC architectures, powering a significant percentage of mobile devices worldwide. Its efficient instruction set and low power consumption have made it the go-to choice for smartphones and tablets.

- **MIPS Architecture:** The MIPS architecture is another classic example of RISC design, known for its simplicity and efficiency. MIPS processors are commonly used in embedded systems, networking equipment, and academic environments.
- **RISC-V:** RISC-V is an open-source RISC architecture that has gained traction in both academia and industry. Its modular design allows for customization, making it suitable for a wide range of applications, from IoT devices to supercomputers.

Conclusion

The RISC philosophy represents a paradigm shift in computer architecture, prioritizing simplicity, efficiency, and performance. By focusing on a reduced instruction set, RISC architectures have paved the way for advancements in processing speed, energy efficiency, and overall computing power. As technology continues to evolve, the principles of RISC will remain integral to the development of future computing systems, reinforcing the importance of innovation in the field of computer architecture.

Redefining Computer Architecture

The landscape of computer architecture underwent a seismic shift with the introduction of Reduced Instruction Set Computing (RISC), a revolutionary philosophy championed by David Patterson. This section delves into how RISC redefined computer architecture, focusing on its core principles, the challenges it addressed, and its lasting impact on modern computing.

Core Principles of RISC

At its essence, RISC architecture is built on the premise that a smaller set of simpler instructions can lead to higher performance. This philosophy contrasts sharply with Complex Instruction Set Computing (CISC), which relies on a larger set of instructions, many of which are rarely used. The key principles of RISC include:

- **Simplicity of Instruction Set:** RISC architectures utilize a limited number of instructions, each designed to execute in a single clock cycle. This simplicity allows for more efficient pipelining, where multiple instruction phases are overlapped in execution.

- **Load/Store Architecture:** RISC separates memory access from computational operations. Only load and store instructions can directly access memory, while all other instructions operate on registers. This reduces the complexity of instruction decoding and execution.

- **Emphasis on Registers:** RISC architectures typically employ a larger number of general-purpose registers. This minimizes the frequency of memory accesses, which are significantly slower than register operations.

- **Fixed-Length Instructions:** Most RISC architectures use fixed-length instructions, simplifying instruction fetching and decoding. This uniformity enhances the efficiency of the instruction pipeline.

These principles collectively contribute to a streamlined and efficient execution model, allowing processors to achieve higher clock speeds and better performance.

Addressing Performance Challenges

Before the advent of RISC, computer architectures faced several performance bottlenecks. The complexity of CISC instructions often led to longer execution times and difficulties in pipelining. By redefining the architecture, Patterson's RISC addressed these challenges effectively:

- **Pipelining Efficiency:** The RISC approach allows for deeper pipelines, where different stages of instruction execution are processed simultaneously. For instance, while one instruction is being executed, another can be decoded, and yet another can be fetched from memory. This parallelism significantly increases throughput.

- **Reduced Instruction Decoding Time:** With a simpler instruction set, RISC processors can decode instructions more rapidly. This reduction in decoding time allows for faster execution cycles, contributing to overall performance gains.

- **Compiler Optimization:** The RISC architecture encourages the development of sophisticated compilers that can optimize code more effectively. Compilers can exploit the simplicity of the instruction set to generate efficient machine code, further enhancing performance.

Examples of RISC Architectures

Several prominent RISC architectures have emerged, each demonstrating the principles of RISC and their impact on computing. Notable examples include:

- **MIPS (Microprocessor without Interlocked Pipeline Stages):** Developed in the 1980s, MIPS is a classic example of RISC architecture. It features a simple instruction set and has been widely used in embedded systems, networking devices, and even gaming consoles.
- **SPARC (Scalable Processor Architecture):** Created by Sun Microsystems, SPARC is another influential RISC architecture. Its design focuses on scalability and performance, making it suitable for high-end server environments.
- **ARM (Advanced RISC Machine):** ARM architecture has become ubiquitous in mobile devices, thanks to its power efficiency and performance. With a focus on low power consumption, ARM processors are widely used in smartphones, tablets, and IoT devices.

The Lasting Impact of RISC

The introduction of RISC has fundamentally altered the trajectory of computer architecture. Its principles have influenced not only the design of modern processors but also the development of new computing paradigms.

- **Modern Processor Design:** Today's processors, including those based on x86 architecture, have adopted many RISC principles, such as pipelining and register-based operations, to enhance performance.
- **Emergence of RISC-V:** The RISC philosophy continues to evolve with the introduction of RISC-V, an open standard instruction set architecture (ISA). RISC-V allows for customization and innovation, fostering a collaborative environment for researchers and developers.
- **Influence on Software Development:** The RISC approach has encouraged the development of more efficient compilers and programming languages, optimizing software performance and resource utilization.

In conclusion, David Patterson's vision in redefining computer architecture through RISC has had a profound and lasting impact on the computing industry. By prioritizing simplicity, efficiency, and performance, RISC has paved the way for modern processor design and continues to shape the future of technology.

The Benefits and Limitations of RISC

Reduced Instruction Set Computing (RISC) has revolutionized the field of computer architecture since its inception. By simplifying the instruction set, RISC aims to enhance performance and efficiency. This section delves into the benefits and limitations of RISC architecture, providing a comprehensive understanding of its impact on modern computing.

Benefits of RISC

1. Simplicity of Instruction Set The fundamental philosophy behind RISC is to use a small, highly optimized instruction set. This simplicity allows for easier decoding and execution of instructions. For example, RISC architectures typically implement a fixed instruction length, which simplifies instruction fetching and decoding.

$$\text{Execution Time} = \text{Instruction Count} \times \text{Cycle Time} \tag{34}$$

This equation illustrates how reducing the instruction count can lead to lower execution times, making RISC processors faster than their Complex Instruction Set Computing (CISC) counterparts.

2. Enhanced Performance through Pipelining RISC architectures are designed to facilitate pipelining, a technique that allows multiple instruction phases to overlap in execution. Since RISC instructions are uniform in length and typically execute in a single cycle, pipelining can be effectively implemented. This leads to a significant increase in throughput.

$$\text{Throughput} = \frac{\text{Number of Instructions}}{\text{Execution Time}} \tag{35}$$

By overlapping instruction execution, RISC processors can achieve higher throughput compared to CISC processors, which often struggle with variable instruction lengths and complex decoding.

3. Improved Compiler Optimization The simplicity of the RISC instruction set allows compilers to generate more efficient code. With fewer instructions to manage, compilers can optimize the use of registers and minimize memory access, leading to better performance.

4. Power Efficiency RISC processors tend to consume less power than CISC processors due to their simpler design and fewer transistors needed for instruction decoding. This is particularly advantageous in mobile and embedded systems where power consumption is critical.

Limitations of RISC

1. Increased Code Size One of the most significant drawbacks of RISC is the potential for increased code size. Since RISC relies on a larger number of simpler instructions, programs may require more instructions to perform the same tasks as those written for CISC architectures. This can lead to higher memory usage.

$$\text{Code Size} = \text{Number of Instructions} \times \text{Average Instruction Size} \tag{36}$$

This equation indicates that while RISC instructions are simpler, the total code size may increase, impacting memory bandwidth and cache efficiency.

2. Complexity in High-Level Language Support RISC architectures may require more complex programming techniques to leverage their full potential. High-level languages may not map directly onto RISC architectures as intuitively as they do on CISC architectures, leading to challenges in software development.

3. Dependency on Compiler Technology The performance benefits of RISC are heavily reliant on advanced compiler technology. If compilers do not efficiently optimize the code for RISC architectures, the advantages of RISC can be diminished. This dependency can create barriers for developers who may not have access to sophisticated compiler tools.

4. Limited Instruction Functionality While RISC's simplicity is a strength, it can also be a limitation. Certain complex operations may require multiple RISC instructions to achieve functionality that a single CISC instruction could handle. For instance, operations like multiplication may need additional instructions to load operands and store results, leading to increased execution time for specific tasks.

Conclusion

In summary, RISC architecture offers a plethora of benefits, including simplicity, enhanced performance through pipelining, improved compiler optimization, and power efficiency. However, these advantages come with trade-offs, such as increased code size, complexity in high-level language support, dependency on compiler technology, and limited instruction functionality. Understanding these benefits and limitations is crucial for appreciating the impact of RISC on the computing landscape and its ongoing evolution in modern technology.

Influencing the Design of Modern Processors

The advent of Reduced Instruction Set Computing (RISC) architecture, spearheaded by David Patterson, has profoundly influenced the design of modern processors. RISC's core philosophy revolves around simplifying the instruction set to increase performance and efficiency, which has become a cornerstone in the evolution of computer architecture.

The RISC Philosophy

At its essence, RISC promotes the idea that a smaller set of instructions can lead to more efficient execution. This is achieved through the use of simple instructions that can be executed within a single clock cycle. The guiding principle can be mathematically represented as:

$$\text{Performance} = \frac{\text{Number of Instructions}}{\text{Execution Time}} \tag{37}$$

By reducing the complexity of instructions, RISC processors can achieve higher throughput, as they can process more instructions in a given time frame.

Design Characteristics of RISC Processors

RISC architecture emphasizes several key design characteristics that have influenced modern processors:

- **Load/Store Architecture:** RISC processors separate memory access from arithmetic operations. Data must be loaded into registers before processing, which simplifies the instruction set and allows for more efficient pipelining.

- **Fixed-Length Instructions:** Most RISC architectures use fixed-length instructions, typically 32 bits. This uniformity simplifies the instruction fetch and decode stages, leading to faster processing.

- **Pipelining:** RISC processors are designed to take advantage of pipelining, where multiple instruction phases are overlapped. This allows for higher instruction throughput and better utilization of processor resources.

- **Register-Based Operations:** RISC architectures utilize a large number of general-purpose registers, minimizing memory access and enhancing speed. For instance, the MIPS architecture includes 32 general-purpose registers.

Impact on Modern Processor Design

The influence of RISC can be seen in various modern processor designs, including ARM, PowerPC, and even x86 architectures, which have adopted RISC principles to enhance performance.

ARM Architecture ARM processors, widely used in mobile devices, embody RISC principles through their efficient instruction set and emphasis on power efficiency. The ARM architecture employs a load/store model, fixed-length instructions, and a rich set of general-purpose registers. The design allows for an efficient execution pipeline, which has been pivotal in the proliferation of smartphones and tablets.

PowerPC Architecture Similarly, the PowerPC architecture, used in both personal computers and embedded systems, integrates RISC principles to optimize performance. It features a highly parallel architecture that supports simultaneous execution of multiple instructions, demonstrating the effectiveness of RISC in achieving high performance.

Challenges and Innovations

While RISC has driven significant advancements in processor design, it has not been without challenges. One notable issue is the increasing complexity of applications that demand more sophisticated processing capabilities. RISC's simplicity can lead to a higher instruction count for complex operations, potentially negating its performance benefits.

To address these challenges, modern RISC architectures have incorporated features traditionally associated with Complex Instruction Set Computing (CISC) architectures, such as:

- **Complex Instructions:** Some RISC designs now include complex instructions that can perform multiple operations in a single instruction, improving efficiency for certain workloads.

- **Out-of-Order Execution:** Many modern RISC processors support out-of-order execution, allowing them to execute instructions as resources become available, rather than strictly adhering to program order. This technique enhances performance by reducing idle time in the pipeline.

- **Speculative Execution:** Speculative execution has also been adopted to further enhance performance. Processors predict the path of branch instructions and execute ahead of time, which can significantly reduce delays caused by branching.

Conclusion

The legacy of RISC architecture, as pioneered by David Patterson, continues to shape the landscape of modern processor design. By emphasizing simplicity, efficiency, and performance, RISC has not only influenced the design of contemporary processors but has also laid the groundwork for future innovations in computing. The principles of RISC remain relevant as the industry grapples with the demands of increasingly complex applications, ensuring that Patterson's vision will endure in the ongoing evolution of technology.

RISC vs CISC: The Ongoing Debate

The debate between Reduced Instruction Set Computer (RISC) and Complex Instruction Set Computer (CISC) architectures has been a defining narrative in the evolution of computer architecture. This section delves into the theoretical underpinnings, practical challenges, and real-world implications of both paradigms, shedding light on their respective advantages and disadvantages.

Theoretical Foundations

At its core, RISC architecture is designed around a small, highly optimized set of instructions, aiming to execute instructions in a single clock cycle. This philosophy promotes simplicity and efficiency, allowing for faster execution times and reduced complexity in instruction decoding. The RISC design principle can be encapsulated in the following equation:

$$\text{Execution Time} = \frac{\text{Number of Instructions}}{\text{Clock Rate}} \times \text{CPI} \tag{38}$$

Where CPI (Cycles Per Instruction) is minimized in RISC architectures due to the uniform instruction length and simplicity.

Conversely, CISC architectures encompass a broader range of instructions, including complex operations that can perform multiple tasks in a single instruction. This leads to a more compact code size, as fewer instructions are needed to perform a given task. The trade-off, however, lies in the increased complexity of the instruction set and the potential for higher CPI:

$$\text{Execution Time} = \frac{\text{Number of Instructions}}{\text{Clock Rate}} \times \text{CPI}_{CISC} \tag{39}$$

Where CPI_{CISC} is typically higher than that of RISC due to the complexity of instruction decoding.

Key Differences

The primary differences between RISC and CISC can be summarized as follows:

- **Instruction Set:** RISC has a limited number of simple instructions, while CISC has a rich set of complex instructions.
- **Instruction Length:** RISC instructions are of fixed length, facilitating easier decoding. CISC instructions can vary in length, complicating the decoding process.
- **Execution Speed:** RISC aims for one instruction per cycle, whereas CISC may take multiple cycles for complex instructions.
- **Memory Usage:** RISC often leads to larger code sizes due to simpler instructions, while CISC can achieve more compact code.

Practical Challenges

Despite their theoretical advantages, both architectures face practical challenges. RISC architectures require more registers to minimize memory access, which can lead to increased silicon area and power consumption. The need for optimizing compilers becomes paramount to fully exploit the capabilities of RISC systems.

On the other hand, CISC architectures, while often more efficient in terms of code size, can suffer from longer execution times due to their complex instruction sets. The overhead of decoding these instructions can lead to inefficiencies, particularly in high-performance scenarios.

Real-World Examples

In practice, the RISC vs. CISC debate can be illustrated through notable examples. The ARM architecture, a prominent RISC design, has gained significant traction in mobile and embedded systems due to its energy efficiency and performance. ARM's simplicity allows for high performance-per-watt, making it ideal for battery-powered devices.

Conversely, x86 architecture, a dominant CISC design, has maintained a stronghold in personal computing. Its ability to execute complex instructions has made it a versatile choice for a wide range of applications, despite its higher power consumption compared to RISC.

The Evolution of the Debate

The lines between RISC and CISC have blurred in recent years. Modern processors often incorporate features from both architectures, leading to hybrid designs. For instance, many contemporary CISC processors implement RISC-like micro-architectural strategies, such as pipelining and superscalar execution, to enhance performance.

Moreover, the emergence of new computing paradigms, such as parallel processing and multicore architectures, has shifted the focus from the RISC vs. CISC debate to optimizing performance through other means. The integration of machine learning and artificial intelligence capabilities into processors has further complicated the landscape, as the requirements for instruction sets evolve.

Conclusion

In conclusion, the RISC vs. CISC debate remains a dynamic and evolving discussion within the field of computer architecture. While RISC offers simplicity and efficiency, CISC provides flexibility and compactness. As technology advances, the need for hybrid approaches and innovative designs continues to shape the future of computing. Understanding the strengths and weaknesses of both architectures is essential for anyone looking to navigate the complexities of modern computer systems.

The Impact of RISC on the Power-Efficiency of Processors

The Reduced Instruction Set Computer (RISC) architecture has fundamentally transformed the landscape of computer processors, particularly in enhancing power efficiency. This section delves into how the principles of RISC contribute to energy savings, the theoretical underpinnings of its design, and practical examples that illustrate its impact on modern computing.

Theoretical Foundations

RISC architecture is predicated on the idea of simplifying the instruction set, allowing for a smaller number of instructions that execute in a single clock cycle. This contrasts sharply with Complex Instruction Set Computing (CISC), which uses a larger set of instructions that may take multiple cycles to execute. The theoretical framework of RISC can be encapsulated in the following key principles:

- **Simplicity of Instruction Set:** RISC uses a limited number of simple instructions, which reduces the complexity of the control logic and allows for faster execution.

- **Fixed Instruction Length:** By employing a uniform instruction length, RISC simplifies the instruction fetch and decode processes, leading to more efficient pipelining.

- **Load/Store Architecture:** RISC architectures typically separate memory access instructions (load/store) from computational instructions, minimizing memory access times and enabling more efficient data handling.

These principles contribute to a decrease in power consumption by reducing the number of transistors that need to switch states during instruction execution. The energy consumed by a processor can be modeled as:

$$E = C \cdot V^2 \cdot f \cdot t \tag{40}$$

where:

- E is the energy consumed,

- C is the capacitance,

- V is the voltage,

- f is the frequency, and

- t is the time the circuit is active.

By minimizing f (frequency) and t (active time) through efficient instruction execution, RISC processors can significantly reduce power consumption.

Power Efficiency in Practice

The RISC architecture has been instrumental in the development of processors for mobile and embedded systems, where power efficiency is paramount. A prime example of this is the ARM architecture, which employs RISC principles and has become the backbone of mobile computing devices.

Case Study: ARM Processors ARM processors exemplify the power efficiency of RISC architecture. In a comparative study of ARM and x86 processors, it was found that ARM processors consume significantly less power while delivering comparable performance for mobile applications. For instance, when executing similar workloads, an ARM Cortex-A72 processor consumes approximately 1.8 watts, while an Intel Core i7 processor can consume upwards of 15 watts under similar conditions.

The power efficiency of ARM processors is further enhanced by their dynamic voltage and frequency scaling (DVFS) capabilities, which allow the processor to adjust its power consumption based on the workload. This adaptability is a direct result of the RISC design philosophy, which emphasizes simplicity and efficiency.

Challenges and Limitations

Despite the advantages of RISC in power efficiency, challenges remain. One significant issue is the potential for increased energy consumption due to the need for more instructions to achieve the same functionality as a CISC processor. For example, a complex operation that might be executed in a single CISC instruction could require multiple RISC instructions, potentially leading to increased power usage in certain scenarios.

Additionally, as applications become more complex, the efficiency gains of RISC can diminish. The overhead of managing multiple simple instructions can lead to increased instruction fetch and decode cycles, which may counteract some of the power savings.

Conclusion

The impact of RISC architecture on the power efficiency of processors is profound and multifaceted. By simplifying the instruction set and optimizing the execution pipeline, RISC has paved the way for energy-efficient computing, particularly in mobile and embedded systems. As the demand for power-efficient solutions continues to rise, RISC principles will undoubtedly play a crucial role in shaping the future of processor design.

In summary, the RISC architecture not only enhances performance through its streamlined design but also leads to significant power savings, making it a cornerstone of modern computing technology. The evolution of processors like ARM showcases the practical benefits of RISC, demonstrating its lasting impact on the industry and its potential for future innovations in power-efficient computing.

Adoption of RISC Architecture by Industry Giants

The RISC (Reduced Instruction Set Computer) architecture, pioneered by David Patterson and his colleagues, revolutionized the computing landscape by promoting a simpler set of instructions that could be executed at high speed. This section delves into how industry giants embraced RISC architecture, transforming their product lines and influencing the broader tech ecosystem.

RISC Architecture: A Brief Overview

At its core, RISC architecture is characterized by a small, highly optimized instruction set designed for efficiency and performance. Unlike its predecessor, CISC (Complex Instruction Set Computer), which featured a large number of instructions that could perform complex tasks, RISC focuses on a limited set of instructions that are executed in a single clock cycle. This design philosophy is encapsulated in the equation:

$$\text{Performance} = \frac{\text{Instructions}}{\text{Cycles} \times \text{Time per Cycle}} \tag{41}$$

By reducing the number of cycles per instruction, RISC processors can achieve higher performance, especially in applications requiring rapid data processing.

Key Industry Adopters

Several industry giants recognized the potential of RISC architecture and adopted it into their product lines:

1. IBM IBM was one of the first major companies to embrace RISC architecture with its RS/6000 line of workstations and servers. The introduction of the POWER architecture in the early 1990s marked a significant shift towards RISC principles. The POWER architecture emphasized parallel processing and high-performance computing, allowing IBM to compete effectively in the server market. The success of POWER processors in high-performance computing environments validated the RISC approach and set a precedent for future designs.

2. **ARM Holdings** ARM Holdings took the RISC architecture to new heights with its ARM processors, which became the backbone of mobile computing. The ARM architecture's energy-efficient design made it ideal for smartphones and tablets, leading to widespread adoption by companies like Apple, Samsung, and Qualcomm. The ARM instruction set is optimized for performance per watt, which is crucial in battery-operated devices. As a result, ARM processors dominate the mobile market, powering billions of devices worldwide.

3. **Sun Microsystems** Sun Microsystems also leveraged RISC architecture with its SPARC (Scalable Processor Architecture) systems. SPARC processors were designed for scalability and high performance, making them suitable for enterprise-level applications. By focusing on RISC principles, Sun was able to deliver systems that excelled in multitasking and data-intensive tasks, solidifying its position in the server and workstation markets during the 1990s.

Impact on the Computing Landscape

The adoption of RISC architecture by these industry giants had far-reaching implications for the computing landscape:

1. **Performance Gains** The transition to RISC architecture resulted in significant performance improvements across various applications. For instance, benchmarks such as SPEC (Standard Performance Evaluation Corporation) demonstrated that RISC processors could outperform their CISC counterparts in many scenarios, particularly in scientific computing and data processing tasks.

2. **Shift in Design Philosophy** The success of RISC architecture prompted a shift in design philosophy across the industry. Companies began to prioritize simplicity, efficiency, and parallelism in their designs. This shift influenced not only the development of new processors but also the software ecosystem, as compilers and programming languages evolved to take advantage of RISC's strengths.

3. **Emergence of New Markets** The energy efficiency of RISC architecture paved the way for the proliferation of mobile devices. As smartphones and tablets became

ubiquitous, the demand for power-efficient processors surged. This trend led to the rise of new markets and opportunities for companies specializing in RISC-based designs, particularly in the realm of Internet of Things (IoT) devices.

Challenges and Considerations

Despite the widespread adoption of RISC architecture, there were challenges and considerations that companies faced:

1. **Compatibility Issues** Transitioning to RISC architecture often posed compatibility challenges for existing software. Many applications were initially designed for CISC processors, requiring significant re-engineering to optimize performance on RISC systems. This challenge highlighted the importance of robust software development tools and compiler optimizations.

2. **Market Competition** The rise of RISC architecture also intensified competition among industry players. Companies had to differentiate their products not only based on performance but also on features, power consumption, and cost. This competition spurred innovation but also led to market fragmentation, with multiple RISC architectures vying for dominance.

Conclusion

The adoption of RISC architecture by industry giants like IBM, ARM Holdings, and Sun Microsystems marked a pivotal moment in computing history. By embracing the principles of RISC, these companies not only improved performance and efficiency but also reshaped the technology landscape. The legacy of RISC continues to influence modern computing, as the principles of simplicity and efficiency remain at the forefront of processor design. As technology evolves, the foundational concepts of RISC architecture will undoubtedly play a crucial role in shaping the future of computing.

Expanding the Reach of RISC into Mobile Devices

The advent of mobile computing has transformed the landscape of technology, making it crucial for architectures to adapt to the constraints and demands of portable devices. RISC (Reduced Instruction Set Computing) architecture, with its streamlined instruction set and efficiency, has emerged as a key player in this domain. This section delves into how RISC has expanded its reach into mobile devices, examining the underlying theory, challenges, and notable examples.

Theoretical Foundations of RISC in Mobile Devices

RISC architecture is characterized by a small set of simple instructions that can be executed within a single clock cycle. This simplicity allows for higher performance and lower power consumption, which are critical factors in mobile devices. The RISC design philosophy emphasizes:

- **Load/Store Architecture:** In RISC, operations are performed only on registers, with memory access limited to load and store instructions. This reduces memory latency and enhances performance, particularly important for mobile applications that require quick data access.
- **Pipelining:** RISC architectures are designed to take advantage of pipelining, where multiple instruction phases are overlapped. This increases instruction throughput and makes efficient use of processor resources.
- **Reduced Complexity:** The simplicity of RISC instructions allows for smaller and more efficient designs, which is beneficial for the compact nature of mobile devices.

The efficiency of RISC architectures aligns perfectly with the needs of mobile devices, which prioritize battery life and performance.

Challenges in Implementing RISC in Mobile Devices

Despite the advantages, several challenges arise when integrating RISC architectures into mobile devices:

- **Power Constraints:** Mobile devices operate on limited battery power. Although RISC is generally power-efficient, the demand for high performance can lead to power spikes that drain batteries quickly.
- **Thermal Management:** Increased performance can result in higher temperatures. Efficient thermal management solutions are necessary to prevent overheating, which can affect device longevity and performance.
- **Software Compatibility:** Transitioning to RISC architectures necessitates the development of compatible software. Many existing applications are optimized for CISC (Complex Instruction Set Computing) architectures, posing a challenge for developers.

Examples of RISC in Mobile Devices

Several notable examples illustrate the successful implementation of RISC architectures in mobile devices:

- **ARM Architecture:** One of the most prominent examples of RISC in mobile computing is the ARM architecture. ARM processors are widely used in smartphones and tablets due to their energy efficiency and high performance. The ARM Cortex series, for instance, employs a RISC design that balances power consumption and processing capabilities, making it ideal for mobile applications.

- **Apple's A-Series Chips:** Apple has leveraged RISC principles in its A-series chips, which power its iPhones and iPads. The A-series chips utilize a custom ARM architecture that optimizes performance for mobile applications while maintaining energy efficiency. The A14 Bionic chip, for example, features a 6-core CPU with a focus on machine learning and graphics performance, showcasing the versatility of RISC in mobile technology.

- **Qualcomm Snapdragon Processors:** Qualcomm's Snapdragon processors, which are integral to many Android devices, also utilize RISC architecture. The Snapdragon series combines RISC with advanced features like integrated GPUs and AI processing capabilities, catering to the diverse needs of modern mobile applications.

The Future of RISC in Mobile Devices

Looking ahead, the expansion of RISC into mobile devices is poised to continue. The rise of IoT (Internet of Things) devices and wearables presents new opportunities for RISC architectures. These devices require efficient processing capabilities while operating under strict power constraints. RISC's inherent advantages make it well-suited for this evolving landscape.

Additionally, the development of RISC-V, an open-source RISC architecture, offers exciting possibilities for innovation in mobile computing. With its customizable nature, RISC-V allows manufacturers to tailor processors to specific applications, further enhancing the efficiency and performance of mobile devices.

In conclusion, the reach of RISC architecture into mobile devices exemplifies the adaptability and relevance of this computing paradigm in a rapidly changing technological environment. As the demand for mobile computing continues to grow, RISC will likely play a pivotal role in shaping the future of portable technology.

$$\text{Performance} = \frac{\text{Instructions}}{\text{Execution Time}} \tag{42}$$

This equation illustrates the fundamental relationship between the number of instructions executed and the time taken, highlighting the efficiency gains that RISC architectures can provide in mobile environments.

RISC-V: Patterson's Next Ambitious Project

The journey of David Patterson in the realm of computer architecture took a significant turn with the introduction of RISC-V, an open standard instruction set architecture (ISA) that emerged as a groundbreaking project in the 21st century. This section delves into the motivations, theoretical underpinnings, and the transformative potential of RISC-V, showcasing Patterson's vision for the future of computing.

The Genesis of RISC-V

RISC-V was conceived at the University of California, Berkeley, where Patterson and his team aimed to create a free and open ISA that could serve as a platform for both academic research and commercial use. The idea stemmed from the realization that existing ISAs, particularly proprietary ones, constrained innovation and accessibility in the field of computer architecture. RISC-V was designed to be modular, allowing users to customize the architecture to fit specific needs without the burden of licensing fees or restrictions.

Theoretical Foundations

The theoretical foundation of RISC-V is rooted in the principles of Reduced Instruction Set Computing (RISC), which emphasizes simplicity and efficiency. The RISC philosophy advocates for a small set of instructions that can execute in a single clock cycle, leading to higher performance and lower power consumption. The RISC-V ISA includes a base set of instructions, with optional extensions for specific functionalities, allowing for flexibility and scalability.

The formal representation of the RISC-V architecture can be described mathematically through its instruction format. For instance, the RISC-V instruction format can be represented as follows:

$$\text{Instruction} = \text{Opcode} + \text{rs1} + \text{rs2} + \text{rd} + \text{funct3} + \text{funct7} \tag{43}$$

Where: - Opcode specifies the operation to be performed. - rs1 and rs2 are the source registers. - rd is the destination register. - funct3 and funct7 provide additional information for the operation.

This modular design allows for a variety of implementations, from low-power microcontrollers to high-performance computing systems.

Challenges and Opportunities

While RISC-V presents numerous advantages, it also faces challenges in adoption and implementation. One significant hurdle is the inertia of existing proprietary architectures that dominate the market. Companies and developers may be reluctant to transition to a new ISA due to the costs associated with retraining, redesigning hardware, and rewriting software.

Moreover, the fragmented nature of the RISC-V ecosystem poses challenges for standardization. Different vendors may implement the architecture differently, leading to compatibility issues. To combat this, the RISC-V Foundation was established to promote the ISA and ensure a cohesive development environment, fostering collaboration among industry leaders and researchers.

Real-World Applications

RISC-V's potential is already being realized in various sectors. For example, companies like SiFive have emerged to provide RISC-V-based processors tailored for specific applications, such as IoT devices and machine learning accelerators. These processors leverage the modularity of RISC-V to deliver optimized performance while maintaining cost-effectiveness.

Additionally, academic institutions are increasingly adopting RISC-V for teaching and research purposes. The open nature of the architecture allows students and researchers to experiment with hardware design and software development without the constraints of proprietary systems. This has led to a surge in innovative projects and collaborations that push the boundaries of what is possible in computer architecture.

The Future of RISC-V

Patterson envisions RISC-V as a catalyst for democratizing access to advanced computing technologies. By providing an open architecture, he aims to empower developers, researchers, and startups to innovate without the barriers imposed by traditional ISAs. This aligns with the broader trend of open-source movements in software and hardware, where collaboration and transparency drive progress.

The future of RISC-V is promising, with ongoing developments in its ecosystem. As more companies adopt RISC-V, the community will grow, leading to a wealth of resources, tools, and libraries that enhance the architecture's usability. Patterson's vision for RISC-V extends beyond mere technical specifications; it encompasses a movement towards a more inclusive and innovative computing landscape.

In conclusion, RISC-V represents David Patterson's next ambitious project, embodying his commitment to advancing computer architecture through open standards. By overcoming challenges and leveraging opportunities, RISC-V has the potential to reshape the future of computing, making it more accessible and adaptable to the needs of a rapidly evolving technological world.

Patterson's Vision for the Future of Computer Architecture

David Patterson, a pioneer in the field of computer architecture, has consistently pushed the boundaries of what is possible in computing. His vision for the future is characterized by a commitment to innovation, accessibility, and sustainability. As we delve into Patterson's forward-thinking ideas, we will explore the theoretical frameworks that underpin his vision, the challenges he anticipates, and the practical examples that illustrate his aspirations.

Theoretical Foundations

At the core of Patterson's vision lies the RISC (Reduced Instruction Set Computer) philosophy, which advocates for simplicity and efficiency in instruction sets. The fundamental theory behind RISC can be summarized in the equation:

$$\text{Performance} = \text{Instructions Per Cycle (IPC)} \times \text{Clock Rate} \tag{44}$$

This equation emphasizes the importance of optimizing both the number of instructions executed per cycle and the clock speed of the processor. Patterson believes that future architectures should continue to refine these parameters, leveraging advancements in semiconductor technology to achieve unprecedented performance levels.

Emerging Technologies

Patterson's vision also incorporates the integration of emerging technologies such as machine learning, quantum computing, and neuromorphic computing. He posits that the next generation of computer architecture must be adaptive and capable of learning from data, thus enhancing performance through intelligent optimization.

For instance, in machine learning, the architecture must support operations like matrix multiplications efficiently. The equation for matrix multiplication, a fundamental operation in many machine learning algorithms, is given by:

$$C_{ij} = \sum_{k=1}^{n} A_{ik} B_{kj} \tag{45}$$

Here, C is the resulting matrix, while A and B are the input matrices. Patterson envisions architectures that can execute such operations in parallel, significantly reducing computation time and power consumption.

Sustainability and Energy Efficiency

As the demand for computing power grows, so does the environmental impact of data centers and computing infrastructure. Patterson advocates for energy-efficient architectures that minimize power consumption without sacrificing performance. He emphasizes the importance of designing processors that can dynamically adjust their power usage based on workload, thereby optimizing energy efficiency.

The relationship between power consumption (P), voltage (V), and frequency (f) can be expressed as:

$$P \propto V^2 \times f \tag{46}$$

This equation highlights how reducing voltage and frequency can significantly decrease power consumption. Patterson's vision includes research into low-power design techniques, such as dynamic voltage and frequency scaling (DVFS), which allow processors to adaptively manage their power usage.

Open Source and Collaboration

Central to Patterson's vision is the belief that open-source principles should govern future developments in computer architecture. He argues that collaboration across the industry can lead to more robust and innovative solutions. The RISC-V architecture serves as a prime example of this philosophy, providing a free and open instruction set architecture that encourages experimentation and adaptation.

Patterson envisions a future where academic institutions, startups, and established tech giants collaborate to develop architectures that are not only powerful but also accessible. This collaborative approach can democratize technology, allowing a broader range of innovators to contribute to the field.

Challenges Ahead

Despite his optimistic outlook, Patterson acknowledges the challenges that lie ahead. The rapid pace of technological advancement often outstrips the ability of regulatory bodies to keep up, leading to ethical dilemmas in areas such as data privacy and security. Patterson advocates for a proactive approach to these issues, encouraging technologists to incorporate ethical considerations into the design process from the outset.

Furthermore, as architectures become more complex, the risk of hardware vulnerabilities increases. Patterson stresses the importance of robust security measures and the need for architectures that can adapt to emerging threats.

Conclusion

David Patterson's vision for the future of computer architecture is a tapestry woven from threads of innovation, collaboration, and ethical responsibility. By continuing to refine the principles of RISC, embracing emerging technologies, prioritizing sustainability, and fostering an open-source culture, Patterson believes that the next generation of computer architects can create systems that are not only powerful but also equitable and responsible. As we stand on the brink of this new era, Patterson's insights will undoubtedly guide the journey ahead, shaping the landscape of computing for years to come.

Chapter Two: Tackling Challenges and Controversies

Section One: The Battle against Proprietary Architecture

The Dominance of Proprietary Systems

In the fast-evolving world of technology, proprietary systems have established a significant foothold, shaping the landscape of computing and influencing the ways in which software and hardware are developed, marketed, and used. Proprietary systems refer to software or hardware that is owned by an individual or a company, with restrictions placed on its use, modification, and distribution. This section explores the nature of proprietary systems, their advantages, their challenges, and the implications for innovation in the tech industry.

Understanding Proprietary Systems

Proprietary systems are characterized by their closed nature, where the source code is not made available to the public. This means that users cannot modify or redistribute the software without permission from the owner. The major players in the tech industry, such as Microsoft, Apple, and Oracle, have built their empires around proprietary systems, creating products that are not only widely used but also generate significant revenue through licensing agreements.

The fundamental equation that underpins the business model of proprietary systems can be represented as:

$$\text{Profit} = \text{Revenue} - \text{Cost} \tag{47}$$

Where: - Revenue is generated from sales and licensing of proprietary software. - Cost includes development, maintenance, and support expenses.

This equation illustrates how companies can maximize profits by controlling the distribution and modification of their products, thereby ensuring a steady stream of income.

Advantages of Proprietary Systems

The dominance of proprietary systems can be attributed to several advantages:

- **Control and Security:** Companies maintain control over their products, which can lead to enhanced security. By limiting access to the source code, they can reduce the risk of vulnerabilities and ensure that users are utilizing the latest, most secure versions of their software.

- **Consistent User Experience:** Proprietary systems often provide a more uniform experience for users, as the company can enforce standards and guidelines for design and functionality. This consistency can enhance user satisfaction and loyalty.

- **Revenue Generation:** Proprietary systems allow companies to monetize their products effectively, creating a sustainable business model that can fund further research and development.

- **Support and Maintenance:** Users of proprietary software typically receive dedicated support and regular updates, which can improve the overall user experience and reduce downtime.

Challenges Associated with Proprietary Systems

Despite their advantages, proprietary systems also face significant challenges:

- **Lack of Flexibility:** Users are often unable to customize proprietary software to meet their specific needs, leading to frustration and inefficiencies. For instance, businesses may find themselves constrained by the limitations of the software they are using.

- **Vendor Lock-In:** Once a company invests in a proprietary system, it may become difficult to switch to alternative solutions due to the costs and complexities involved. This dependency can stifle innovation and create barriers to entry for new competitors.

- **Limited Collaboration:** The closed nature of proprietary systems can hinder collaboration among developers. Without access to the source code, it becomes challenging to build upon existing technologies or integrate new features, ultimately slowing down progress in the industry.

Examples of Proprietary Systems

Several well-known proprietary systems exemplify the dominance of this model:

- **Microsoft Windows:** As one of the most widely used operating systems globally, Windows is a prime example of a proprietary system. Users must purchase licenses to use the software, and modifications are restricted.

- **Apple macOS:** Similar to Windows, macOS is a proprietary operating system that is tightly controlled by Apple. The company dictates the hardware on which macOS can run, creating a closed ecosystem that enhances user experience but limits flexibility.

- **Oracle Database:** As a leading database management system, Oracle's software is proprietary, requiring organizations to pay for licenses and support. This model has allowed Oracle to dominate the enterprise database market while creating significant barriers for competitors.

Conclusion

The dominance of proprietary systems in the tech industry has profound implications for innovation, competition, and user experience. While these systems offer advantages such as control, security, and revenue generation, they also present challenges that can stifle flexibility and collaboration. As the industry continues to evolve, the tension between proprietary systems and open-source alternatives will shape the future of technology. Understanding this dynamic is essential for navigating the complexities of the computing landscape and for recognizing the need for a more inclusive approach to technological development.

Patterson's Advocacy for Open Source

David Patterson's journey in the tech world is marked not only by his groundbreaking contributions to computer architecture but also by his staunch advocacy for open-source technology. In a landscape dominated by proprietary systems, Patterson emerged as a vocal proponent of open-source principles, emphasizing the importance of accessibility, collaboration, and community-driven innovation.

The Philosophy of Open Source

At its core, the open-source movement champions the idea that software should be freely available for anyone to use, modify, and distribute. This philosophy stands in stark contrast to proprietary models, where software is tightly controlled and access is restricted. Patterson recognized that open-source software could democratize technology, allowing individuals and organizations, regardless of their resources, to leverage powerful tools for innovation.

The open-source model aligns with the principles of transparency and collaboration, fostering a community of developers who contribute their expertise to improve software collectively. Patterson often cited the benefits of this collaborative approach in his talks and writings, arguing that it leads to more robust, secure, and versatile software solutions.

Patterson's Initiatives

One of Patterson's most notable contributions to the open-source movement is his role in founding the RISC-V Foundation in 2015. RISC-V, an open standard instruction set architecture (ISA), embodies Patterson's vision of accessible technology. By providing a free and open ISA, RISC-V allows researchers, educators, and companies to experiment with and develop their own processors without the burden of licensing fees or proprietary restrictions.

$$\text{RISC-V ISA} = \text{Base Integer Instruction Set} + \text{Optional Extensions} \tag{48}$$

This equation illustrates the modular nature of RISC-V, where the base instruction set can be extended with optional features, enabling users to tailor the architecture to their specific needs.

Challenges in Promoting Open Source

Despite its advantages, Patterson faced significant challenges in advocating for open-source technology. The dominance of proprietary systems created a competitive environment where established companies were reluctant to embrace open-source principles. Patterson often encountered skepticism from industry leaders who viewed open-source as a threat to their business models.

For instance, during the early days of RISC-V, Patterson faced pushback from companies heavily invested in proprietary architectures. These companies argued that open-source initiatives could undermine their market position and intellectual property rights. Patterson countered these arguments by highlighting the long-term benefits of open-source collaboration, including faster innovation cycles and the potential for new markets to emerge.

Real-World Examples

Patterson's advocacy for open-source has yielded tangible results. The RISC-V architecture has gained traction in academia and industry, with numerous universities incorporating it into their curricula, fostering a new generation of engineers proficient in open-source technologies. Companies such as Western Digital and NVIDIA have also adopted RISC-V for various applications, from embedded systems to advanced computing.

Moreover, Patterson's influence extends beyond RISC-V. He has been a key figure in promoting open-source tools and platforms that facilitate research and development. For example, his support for the Open Compute Project encourages collaboration among hardware developers to create open designs for data center hardware, further exemplifying his commitment to open-source principles.

The Ethical Dimension of Open Source

Patterson's advocacy for open-source technology also encompasses ethical considerations. He believes that technology should be accessible to all, particularly in developing countries where resources may be limited. By promoting open-source solutions, Patterson aims to bridge the digital divide and empower individuals and communities to harness technology for their benefit.

In his speeches, Patterson often emphasizes the role of open-source in fostering inclusivity and diversity within the tech industry. He argues that when technology is open and accessible, it encourages participation from a broader range of voices, leading to more innovative and representative solutions.

Looking Ahead

As the tech landscape continues to evolve, Patterson remains a steadfast advocate for open-source technology. His vision for the future includes a world where open-source principles are integrated into the fabric of technological development, ensuring that innovation is driven by collaboration rather than competition.

In conclusion, David Patterson's advocacy for open source represents a significant shift in the tech industry's approach to software development and collaboration. By championing open-source principles, Patterson not only advanced the field of computer architecture but also paved the way for a more inclusive and equitable technological future. His legacy serves as a reminder of the power of community-driven innovation and the importance of making technology accessible to all.

Tensions with Industry Leaders

In the fast-paced world of technology, the emergence of new ideas often triggers friction among established industry leaders. David Patterson's advocacy for Reduced Instruction Set Computing (RISC) architecture not only revolutionized computer design but also placed him at the center of a storm of tensions with powerful entities in the tech landscape. This section delves into the dynamics of these conflicts, exploring the implications for Patterson, RISC, and the broader computing industry.

The Established Order

At the heart of the tension was the dominance of Complex Instruction Set Computing (CISC) architectures, which had long been the standard in the industry. Companies like Intel and IBM had invested heavily in CISC designs, which offered a rich set of instructions aimed at optimizing performance for complex tasks. The prevailing belief was that more instructions meant better performance. However, Patterson's research challenged this notion, suggesting that a simpler instruction set could lead to higher performance through increased efficiency and speed.

$$\text{Performance} \propto \frac{\text{Clock Speed} \times \text{Instructions}}{\text{Cycles per Instruction}} \tag{49}$$

This equation illustrates the core of Patterson's argument: by reducing the cycles per instruction, RISC could achieve higher performance despite having fewer instructions. Yet, this radical departure from established norms was not without backlash.

Industry Backlash

As Patterson began to publish his findings and advocate for RISC, he faced significant resistance from industry leaders who perceived his work as a direct threat to their business models. The initial reception of RISC was met with skepticism, as many believed that the existing CISC architecture was sufficient for the needs of the market. This skepticism was fueled by the fear that adopting RISC would require a complete overhaul of existing systems and processes, leading to substantial financial investments.

For instance, during the early 1980s, Patterson's work at the University of California, Berkeley, brought him into direct conflict with Intel. The company's executives were wary of the potential for RISC to disrupt their sales of CISC processors. In response, Intel's marketing campaigns emphasized the advantages of CISC, often dismissing RISC as an academic curiosity rather than a viable alternative.

Public Debates and Controversies

The tensions escalated into public debates, with Patterson often finding himself in the crosshairs of industry criticism. In conferences and journals, industry leaders would question the practicality of RISC, arguing that the existing CISC designs were more than capable of handling consumer demands. They claimed that RISC oversimplified the complexities of real-world applications, where a more extensive instruction set was necessary to achieve optimal performance.

These debates were not merely academic; they had real-world implications. Companies that adhered to CISC were reluctant to invest in RISC technologies, fearing that it could jeopardize their market position. Patterson's advocacy for RISC thus became a rallying point for those who believed in innovation versus those who clung to tradition.

The GPL Revolution

Amidst the growing tensions, a pivotal moment arose with the advent of the General Public License (GPL) revolution. Patterson, seeing the potential for RISC to thrive in an open-source environment, advocated for the development of RISC architectures that could be freely shared and modified. This stance put him at odds with proprietary giants who relied on closed systems to maintain their competitive edge.

The GPL movement, championed by figures like Richard Stallman, emphasized the importance of open-source software and hardware, arguing that collaboration and accessibility would drive innovation. Patterson's support for these ideals positioned him as a leader in the movement toward open architecture, further intensifying the tensions with industry leaders who viewed this as a direct challenge to their business models.

The RISC-V Foundation

The culmination of these tensions led to the formation of the RISC-V Foundation in 2015, an initiative aimed at promoting open standards for RISC architectures. Patterson's involvement with this foundation marked a significant turning point, as it provided a platform for collaboration among companies, researchers, and developers interested in RISC. The foundation's mission was to create an open-source instruction set architecture that would allow for innovation without the barriers imposed by proprietary systems.

However, this initiative did not come without its own set of challenges. Industry leaders, still clinging to their CISC architectures, viewed the RISC-V Foundation with skepticism. They questioned the viability of an open-source approach in a market dominated by proprietary technologies. This skepticism manifested in various ways, from reluctance to adopt RISC-V in new products to active lobbying against its acceptance in industry standards.

The Road Ahead

Despite the tensions, Patterson's vision for RISC and the ongoing evolution of computer architecture continued to gain traction. As more companies began to recognize the benefits of RISC, particularly in the context of power efficiency and performance, the landscape began to shift. Industry giants such as Google and NVIDIA started to embrace RISC-V, validating Patterson's long-held belief in the architecture's potential.

The tension between Patterson and industry leaders serves as a reminder of the challenges faced by innovators in any field. As new technologies emerge, they often disrupt established paradigms, leading to resistance from those who benefit from the status quo. Patterson's journey illustrates the importance of perseverance in the face of adversity, as well as the power of collaboration in driving technological advancement.

In conclusion, the tensions between David Patterson and industry leaders highlight the complexities of innovation in technology. As RISC architecture continued to gain recognition, the initial resistance transformed into a broader acceptance, paving the way for a new era in computing. Patterson's commitment to open standards and collaboration ultimately reshaped the industry, proving that sometimes, the most revolutionary ideas come from challenging the established order.

The GPL Revolution

The General Public License (GPL) represents a monumental shift in the landscape of software licensing, positioning itself as a cornerstone of the open-source movement. This section delves into the principles of the GPL, its implications for the tech industry, and the revolutionary changes it has catalyzed, particularly in the context of David Patterson's advocacy for open-source technologies.

Understanding the GPL

The GPL, created by Richard Stallman in 1989, is a copyleft license that allows software to be freely used, modified, and distributed. The fundamental premise of the GPL is that software should be accessible to everyone, ensuring that users have the freedom to run, study, change, and distribute the software. The license operates on the principle of reciprocity, which means that any derivative work must also be distributed under the same license terms. This ensures that improvements made to the software remain available to the public, fostering a collaborative development environment.

$$\text{Freedom to Use} + \text{Freedom to Modify} + \text{Freedom to Distribute} + \text{Freedom to Share Improve} \tag{50}$$

This equation encapsulates the essence of the GPL, highlighting how each freedom contributes to the overarching goal of open-source software.

The Impact of the GPL on Proprietary Systems

Before the GPL, the software industry was dominated by proprietary systems, where companies held exclusive rights over their code, stifling innovation and collaboration. The GPL challenged this norm by empowering developers and users alike. Patterson recognized the potential of the GPL to democratize technology, advocating for open-source solutions that could compete with proprietary architectures.

The GPL's influence became particularly evident in the rise of the Linux operating system, which was released under the GPL in 1991. This event marked a turning point, as Linux grew from a small project into a global phenomenon, leading to widespread adoption in various industries. The success of Linux demonstrated that a collaborative, open-source approach could rival and even surpass proprietary systems in terms of performance, security, and flexibility.

Challenges Faced by the GPL

Despite its successes, the GPL faced significant challenges, particularly from industry leaders who viewed open-source software as a threat to their business models. Companies like Microsoft initially dismissed the GPL as a fringe movement, but as open-source software gained traction, they began to recognize its implications. The GPL's requirement for sharing source code clashed with the proprietary ethos, leading to tensions that would shape the future of software development.

One notable example of this tension is the infamous "Halloween Documents," a series of internal memos from Microsoft that expressed concern over the growing influence of open-source software and the GPL. These documents revealed the company's strategy to combat the open-source movement, highlighting the fear that the GPL instilled in proprietary software vendors.

Patterson's Advocacy for Open Source

David Patterson emerged as a vocal advocate for open-source principles, recognizing the GPL as a vehicle for innovation and collaboration. He argued that the GPL allowed for a more equitable technological landscape, where smaller companies and individual developers could compete with industry giants. Patterson's work on RISC architecture exemplified this ethos, as he encouraged the adoption of open standards that would enable a broader range of contributors to participate in the development process.

Patterson's involvement in the RISC-V project further solidified his commitment to open-source principles. RISC-V, an open standard instruction set architecture, embodies the GPL's spirit by allowing anyone to implement, modify, and extend the architecture without the constraints of proprietary licenses. This initiative has attracted a diverse community of developers, researchers, and companies, fostering innovation in a way that proprietary systems cannot replicate.

The Future of Open Source and the GPL

As the tech industry continues to evolve, the relevance of the GPL remains steadfast. The rise of cloud computing, artificial intelligence, and machine learning has introduced new challenges and opportunities for open-source software.

Companies are increasingly recognizing the value of collaboration and shared knowledge, leading to a growing acceptance of open-source licenses.

Patterson's vision for the future of computer architecture aligns with the principles of the GPL. He believes that the collaborative nature of open-source development can drive advancements in technology, making it more accessible and inclusive. The GPL revolution has laid the groundwork for a new era of innovation, where the power of collective intelligence can be harnessed to tackle complex challenges.

In conclusion, the GPL revolution represents a fundamental shift in the software industry, challenging the status quo of proprietary systems and promoting a culture of collaboration and transparency. David Patterson's advocacy for open-source technologies has played a crucial role in this movement, shaping the future of computing and inspiring the next generation of technologists to embrace the principles of freedom and accessibility in their work.

$$\text{Open Source Revolution} = \text{GPL} + \text{Community Collaboration} + \text{Innovation} \Rightarrow \text{A New Era} \tag{51}$$

The equation above illustrates how the GPL, combined with community collaboration and innovation, has ushered in a new era in technology, one that David Patterson has been instrumental in shaping.

The RISC-V Foundation: Challenging the Status Quo

The RISC-V Foundation emerged as a pivotal player in the landscape of computer architecture, championing the principles of openness and accessibility in a domain often dominated by proprietary systems. Founded in 2015, the RISC-V Foundation was established to promote the RISC-V instruction set architecture (ISA) and to foster a collaborative ecosystem that encourages innovation and inclusivity in technology development.

The Vision Behind RISC-V

At the heart of the RISC-V initiative lies a vision for a free and open ISA that allows designers to create custom processors without the constraints of licensing fees and proprietary restrictions. This radical departure from traditional models, where companies like Intel and ARM held significant sway over the architecture landscape, sought to democratize access to advanced computing technologies.

The RISC-V ISA is designed with simplicity and modularity in mind, enabling a wide range of applications from embedded systems to high-performance computing. The foundational philosophy of RISC-V can be summarized as follows:

$$\text{RISC-V} = \text{Simplicity} + \text{Flexibility} + \text{Open Standards} \tag{52}$$

This equation illustrates how RISC-V strives to balance simplicity in design with the flexibility required for diverse applications, all while adhering to open standards that empower developers.

Challenging Industry Norms

The establishment of the RISC-V Foundation posed a direct challenge to the status quo of proprietary architectures. Traditionally, companies invested heavily in the development of custom architectures, often resulting in a closed ecosystem where innovation was stifled by licensing agreements and intellectual property constraints. The rise of RISC-V has catalyzed a shift in this paradigm, encouraging a culture of collaboration and shared knowledge.

One of the key problems that RISC-V addresses is the high cost of entry for new companies and startups in the semiconductor industry. By providing an open-source ISA, the RISC-V Foundation allows innovators to develop their own hardware without the burden of costly licenses. This has led to a burgeoning community of developers and researchers who can contribute to the evolution of the architecture.

Real-World Examples of RISC-V Adoption

Several notable organizations and projects have embraced RISC-V, demonstrating its viability as a competitive alternative to established architectures. For instance, Western Digital announced its commitment to RISC-V as the foundation for its future storage devices, aiming to leverage the open architecture for greater efficiency and performance. Similarly, companies like NVIDIA and Google have also begun exploring RISC-V for various applications, signaling a growing acceptance of the architecture in mainstream tech.

In academia, numerous universities have integrated RISC-V into their computer science curricula, allowing students to learn about modern processor design in an open environment. This educational approach fosters a new generation of engineers who are well-versed in open-source principles and capable of pushing the boundaries of what's possible in computing.

The Ethical Dimension of Open Source

The RISC-V Foundation's commitment to open-source principles also raises important ethical considerations. By promoting an open ISA, the foundation advocates for transparency and accountability in technology development. This is particularly relevant in an era where concerns about data privacy and security are paramount. Open-source architectures allow for greater scrutiny of the underlying technology, enabling developers and users to identify and mitigate potential vulnerabilities.

Furthermore, the RISC-V Foundation emphasizes inclusivity, encouraging participation from diverse groups within the tech community. This approach not only enriches the development process but also ensures that the resulting technologies serve a broader range of societal needs.

Looking Ahead: The Future of RISC-V

As the RISC-V Foundation continues to grow, its impact on the computing landscape is expected to expand. The foundation is actively working to establish a robust ecosystem of tools, software, and hardware that supports RISC-V development. Initiatives such as the RISC-V Software Ecosystem and the RISC-V Compliance Program are designed to ensure that RISC-V implementations meet high standards of performance and compatibility.

In conclusion, the RISC-V Foundation stands as a testament to the power of open-source collaboration in challenging entrenched industry norms. By fostering an environment where innovation can thrive without the constraints of proprietary systems, RISC-V is poised to redefine the future of computer architecture. As more organizations and individuals join the movement, the potential for groundbreaking advancements in technology is limitless.

$$\text{Future of RISC-V} = \text{Collaboration} + \text{Innovation} + \text{Accessibility} \tag{53}$$

This equation encapsulates the foundation's aspirations, highlighting its role as a catalyst for change in the tech industry.

Patterson's Crusade for Accessible Technology

In the fast-paced world of technology, the notion of accessibility often becomes an afterthought, overshadowed by the allure of cutting-edge innovations and proprietary advancements. However, David Patterson emerged as a beacon of hope, advocating for the democratization of technology. His crusade for accessible technology was not merely an ambition; it was a mission rooted in the belief that everyone, regardless of their socio-economic background, should have the opportunity to harness the power of computing.

Theoretical Underpinnings of Accessibility

At the heart of Patterson's advocacy lies the theory of *Universal Design,* which emphasizes creating products and environments that are usable by all people, to the greatest extent possible, without the need for adaptation or specialized design. This approach aligns with the principles of *Inclusive Design,* which takes into account the diverse needs of users, ensuring that technology serves a wider audience. Patterson's work in this domain reflects a profound understanding of the socio-technical landscape, where technology intersects with human experience.

Challenges in Achieving Accessibility

Despite the noble intentions behind accessible technology, numerous challenges persist. One significant barrier is the *digital divide,* a term that refers to the gap between those who have easy access to digital technology and those who do not. This divide is often exacerbated by socio-economic factors, geographical disparities, and educational inequalities. Patterson recognized that for technology to be truly accessible, it must be affordable and user-friendly, especially for underserved communities.

Another challenge is the *proprietary nature* of many technological solutions. Companies often prioritize profit over accessibility, creating systems that are locked behind paywalls and technical jargon that can alienate potential users. Patterson's advocacy for open-source solutions served as a countermeasure to this trend, promoting transparency and collaborative development as means to foster inclusivity.

Patterson's Initiatives for Accessibility

Patterson's commitment to accessible technology manifested in several key initiatives. One notable example is his involvement with the *RISC-V Foundation,* which champions open-source hardware. By promoting a free and open architecture, Patterson aimed to lower the barriers to entry for developers and researchers, particularly in academic and non-profit sectors. This initiative was pivotal in empowering a global community of innovators who could build upon RISC-V without the constraints of proprietary systems.

Moreover, Patterson's work in academia emphasized the importance of *educational outreach*. He believed that equipping the next generation with the skills needed to navigate the tech landscape was essential for fostering an inclusive environment. Programs that introduced computer science to underrepresented groups in schools and communities became a cornerstone of his efforts. For instance, Patterson supported initiatives that provided coding workshops and resources in low-income neighborhoods, ensuring that children from diverse backgrounds could engage with technology from an early age.

Real-World Examples of Accessible Technology

To illustrate the impact of Patterson's crusade, consider the development of *RISC-V* processors in educational institutions. By leveraging open-source designs, universities could provide students with hands-on experience in computer architecture without the burden of expensive licensing fees. This approach not only democratized access to advanced computational resources but also fostered a spirit of innovation among students who might not have otherwise had such opportunities.

Another example is the rise of *assistive technologies* that embody Patterson's principles of accessibility. Tools such as speech recognition software and screen readers have transformed the way individuals with disabilities interact with technology. Patterson's advocacy for open-source solutions in this space has encouraged the development of customizable tools that cater to specific needs, furthering the mission of inclusivity.

The Ethical Dimension of Accessibility

Patterson's crusade also delved into the ethical implications of technology. He recognized that accessibility is not just a technical challenge but a moral imperative. The ethical dimension of accessible technology involves ensuring that advancements do not exacerbate existing inequalities. Patterson's philosophy was clear: technology should uplift and empower, not entrench disparities.

In his public speeches and writings, he often highlighted the responsibility of technologists to consider the broader societal impact of their innovations. This perspective resonated with many in the tech community, sparking discussions about the role of ethics in technology development. Patterson's influence encouraged a generation of programmers and engineers to prioritize accessibility as a core value in their work.

Looking Ahead: The Future of Accessible Technology

As we look to the future, Patterson's crusade for accessible technology remains more relevant than ever. The rapid evolution of technology presents both opportunities and challenges in achieving inclusivity. Emerging fields such as artificial intelligence and machine learning hold the potential to revolutionize accessibility, but they also pose risks if not approached thoughtfully.

Patterson's vision for the future emphasizes the need for ongoing collaboration between technologists, policymakers, and communities to ensure that advancements benefit everyone. By fostering an ecosystem that values open-source principles and ethical considerations, the tech industry can move closer to realizing the goal of universal accessibility.

In conclusion, David Patterson's crusade for accessible technology is a testament to his belief in the power of computing to transform lives. His advocacy for open-source solutions, educational outreach, and ethical considerations has laid a foundation for a more inclusive technological landscape. As we continue to navigate the complexities of the digital age, Patterson's legacy serves as a guiding light for those committed to making technology accessible to all.

The Ethical Dimension of Open Source

The ethical dimension of open source software (OSS) is a multifaceted topic that encompasses issues of accessibility, collaboration, and the implications of software freedom in a digital age. Open source advocates argue that software should be freely available for anyone to use, modify, and distribute, while proprietary software models often restrict access and control. This section explores the ethical considerations surrounding open source, emphasizing its role in democratizing technology and fostering innovation.

Accessibility and Inclusivity

One of the primary ethical arguments for open source is its potential to enhance accessibility. By allowing users to access source code, OSS promotes inclusivity, enabling individuals from diverse backgrounds to participate in technology development. This inclusivity is particularly crucial in developing countries where access to proprietary software can be prohibitively expensive. For instance, the widespread adoption of the Linux operating system in educational institutions has provided students with a cost-effective platform to learn programming and computer science.

Collaboration and Community Building

Open source software fosters a collaborative environment that encourages knowledge sharing and community engagement. The ethos of open source is rooted in the belief that collective effort leads to better outcomes. This collaborative spirit is exemplified by projects like the Apache HTTP Server, which has become one of the most widely used web servers globally, largely due to contributions from a diverse group of developers. The ethical implications of this collaboration extend beyond mere technical advancements; they promote a culture of mutual respect and shared ownership.

The Right to Modify and Control

The freedom to modify and control software is a fundamental tenet of the open source movement. This principle aligns with the ethical stance that users should have autonomy over the technology they use. Richard Stallman, a prominent advocate for free software, famously stated, "The user should be in control of the program, not the other way around." This philosophy raises questions about the ethical responsibilities of developers and corporations. When proprietary software companies impose restrictions on users, they limit individual freedoms and can create dependencies that may be detrimental in the long run.

Transparency and Accountability

Transparency is another critical ethical aspect of open source. By making source code publicly available, OSS projects allow for scrutiny and validation by anyone in the community. This transparency fosters accountability and can lead to higher security standards, as vulnerabilities are more likely to be identified and addressed. For example, the OpenSSL project, which provides cryptographic functions for secure communications, faced significant scrutiny after the Heartbleed bug was discovered. The public nature of the project allowed for a rapid response and the implementation of fixes, highlighting the ethical imperative of maintaining secure software.

Challenges and Ethical Dilemmas

Despite the many benefits of open source, there are ethical dilemmas that arise within the movement. One significant challenge is the potential for misuse of open source software. While the freedom to modify software is a core principle, it can also lead to the creation of malicious applications. For instance, tools developed for legitimate purposes, such as penetration testing, can be repurposed for unethical hacking. This duality raises questions about the responsibility of developers and the need for ethical guidelines within the open source community.

The Role of Licensing

Licensing plays a crucial role in shaping the ethical landscape of open source software. Different open source licenses, such as the GNU General Public License (GPL) and the MIT License, embody varying philosophies regarding user freedoms and obligations. The GPL, for example, requires that derivative works also be open source, promoting a cycle of sharing and collaboration. In contrast, the MIT License allows for proprietary use, which can lead to ethical concerns about the commercialization of open source projects without contributing back to the community. Understanding these licenses is essential for developers who wish to navigate the ethical implications of their work effectively.

Conclusion

In conclusion, the ethical dimension of open source software is a complex interplay of accessibility, collaboration, autonomy, transparency, and accountability. While open source has the potential to democratize technology and foster innovation, it also presents challenges that require careful consideration. As the tech landscape continues to evolve, the ethical implications of open source will remain a vital area of discussion, urging developers, corporations, and users alike to reflect on their roles in shaping a more equitable digital future.

Pushback and Resistance from Competitors

The journey of David Patterson and the RISC (Reduced Instruction Set Computing) architecture has not been without its fair share of challenges and pushback from competitors entrenched in the existing paradigms of computer architecture. The introduction of RISC was a significant shift in the way processors were designed and utilized, and as with any revolutionary idea, it faced substantial resistance from established industry leaders who were invested in the status quo.

The Established Norm: CISC Dominance

Before RISC emerged, the dominant architecture was CISC (Complex Instruction Set Computing). CISC architectures, such as those developed by Intel and IBM, were characterized by a large set of instructions that could execute complex operations in a single command. This design philosophy was deeply embedded in the industry, with companies having significant investments in CISC technology and a workforce trained to optimize and work within its framework. The entrenched nature of CISC made any shift towards a radically different architecture like RISC a daunting challenge.

Resistance from Industry Giants

As Patterson and his collaborators began to advocate for RISC, they encountered fierce resistance from several industry giants. Companies like Intel and Motorola, which had built their empires on CISC designs, viewed RISC as a direct threat to their market dominance. The pushback was multifaceted:

1. **Technical Skepticism**: Many engineers and decision-makers in established companies were initially skeptical of RISC's claims. They argued that the performance benefits were overstated and that the existing CISC architectures were more efficient for complex applications. This skepticism was rooted in the fear of change and the substantial investments already made in CISC technology.

2. **Marketing and Misinformation**: Competitors often resorted to marketing campaigns aimed at discrediting RISC. They emphasized the supposed limitations of RISC, such as its reduced instruction set leading to increased code size, which they claimed could negatively impact performance in certain applications.

3. **Legal and Competitive Tactics**: In some instances, competitors engaged in legal battles to protect their intellectual property and market share. They sought to undermine RISC's acceptance in the industry through litigation and lobbying efforts, attempting to sway public opinion against it.

Theoretical Underpinnings of RISC vs. CISC

The theoretical foundation of RISC is grounded in the idea of simplicity and efficiency. RISC architectures utilize a smaller set of simple instructions that can execute in a single clock cycle, as opposed to CISC architectures that may require multiple cycles for complex instructions. This is formally represented as:

$$\text{Execution Time} = \text{Number of Instructions} \times \text{Cycles per Instruction} \tag{54}$$

In RISC, the goal is to minimize the Cycles per Instruction by using a simpler instruction set, thus potentially leading to lower execution times overall. However, the pushback from competitors often centered on the argument that the complexity of tasks in real-world applications could not be efficiently handled by RISC without incurring other costs, such as increased memory usage.

Examples of Pushback

Several notable instances exemplify the resistance Patterson faced:

- **Intel's Response**: As RISC gained traction, Intel launched initiatives to bolster its own CISC architectures, introducing features that aimed to mimic some benefits of RISC, such as pipelining and superscalar execution. This was a clear acknowledgment of RISC's influence but also an attempt to retain CISC's market share.

- **The RISC vs. CISC Debate**: The academic and industry debates surrounding RISC versus CISC became a battleground. Conferences and journals were filled with papers either supporting RISC's advantages or defending CISC's established methodologies. This public discourse often mirrored the competitive tensions, with proponents of each architecture fiercely defending their positions.

Patterson's Resilience and Adaptation

Despite the pushback, Patterson's resilience and commitment to the principles of RISC ultimately led to its acceptance in the industry. He and his collaborators focused on demonstrating the practical benefits of RISC through research, publications, and collaborations with key players in the tech industry. They conducted rigorous benchmarks that showcased RISC's performance advantages, particularly in specific applications such as graphics processing and scientific computing.

Furthermore, Patterson's advocacy for open-source principles allowed RISC to gain traction among smaller companies and startups that were looking for alternatives to the proprietary CISC systems. This grassroots support helped to create a community around RISC that countered the resistance from larger competitors.

Conclusion

The pushback and resistance from competitors were significant hurdles in the journey of RISC and David Patterson. However, the determination to challenge the status quo, backed by theoretical foundations and practical demonstrations, allowed RISC to carve out its place in the computing landscape. This chapter of Patterson's story highlights not only the challenges faced by innovators in technology but also the resilience required to overcome them and the importance of adaptability in the face of adversity.

The Impact of the RISC-V Movement

The RISC-V movement represents a revolutionary shift in the landscape of computer architecture, founded on principles of openness, collaboration, and accessibility. Emerging from the pioneering work of David Patterson and his colleagues, RISC-V is an open standard instruction set architecture (ISA) that has gained traction across academia and industry. This section delves into the multifaceted impact of the RISC-V movement, emphasizing its theoretical underpinnings, practical challenges, and real-world examples.

Theoretical Foundations

RISC-V is built upon the Reduced Instruction Set Computing (RISC) philosophy, which advocates for a simplified set of instructions that can be executed within a single clock cycle. This approach contrasts sharply with Complex Instruction Set Computing (CISC), which employs a more intricate instruction set. The theoretical advantages of RISC-V include:

$$\text{Performance} \propto \frac{\text{Clock Rate} \times \text{Instructions Per Cycle}}{\text{Cycles Per Instruction}} \tag{55}$$

This equation illustrates that optimizing for instructions per cycle (IPC) and clock rate can lead to enhanced performance, a fundamental principle behind RISC architectures.

Addressing Industry Challenges

Despite its advantages, the adoption of RISC-V has not been without challenges. The proprietary nature of existing architectures like x86 and ARM poses significant barriers to entry. Industry giants have historically dominated the market, creating a landscape where innovation is stifled by licensing fees and restrictive agreements. The RISC-V movement confronts these challenges head-on by promoting an open-source model, allowing developers to implement the architecture without incurring costs or legal restrictions.

One of the core problems in the transition to RISC-V is the need for robust ecosystem support. Developers and companies must invest in tools, compilers, and software libraries that are compatible with RISC-V. The RISC-V Foundation has been instrumental in fostering this ecosystem, collaborating with universities, startups, and established tech companies to create a comprehensive suite of resources.

Examples of RISC-V Implementation

The impact of the RISC-V movement is evident in various sectors, from embedded systems to high-performance computing. Notable implementations include:

- **SiFive:** A startup that has leveraged RISC-V to create customizable processors tailored to specific applications. Their Freedom U540 processor, based on RISC-V, has been employed in various consumer electronics, showcasing the architecture's versatility.
- **Western Digital:** The company announced plans to adopt RISC-V for its data storage devices, highlighting the architecture's scalability and efficiency in handling large volumes of data.
- **NVIDIA:** As part of their commitment to open standards, NVIDIA has explored RISC-V for certain AI workloads, illustrating the architecture's potential in high-performance computing environments.

Impact on Education and Research

RISC-V has also transformed the educational landscape, providing a platform for students and researchers to engage with cutting-edge technology without the constraints of proprietary systems. Universities worldwide have integrated RISC-V into their curricula, allowing students to learn about computer architecture and design using an open-source framework. This accessibility fosters innovation and encourages the next generation of engineers to contribute to the field.

The Global Movement Towards Open Standards

The RISC-V movement is more than just a technical initiative; it embodies a broader cultural shift towards open standards in technology. The principles of collaboration and transparency resonate with a growing community of developers who seek to democratize access to technology. The RISC-V Foundation has played a pivotal role in uniting stakeholders across the globe, hosting conferences and workshops to promote knowledge sharing and collaboration.

In conclusion, the impact of the RISC-V movement extends far beyond its technical specifications. It challenges the status quo of proprietary architectures, promotes an open-source ethos, and inspires a new generation of technologists. As RISC-V continues to gain momentum, its influence on the computing industry is poised to reshape the future of technology, making it more inclusive, innovative, and accessible.

Looking Ahead: The Future of Open Source Computer Architecture

The future of open source computer architecture is poised for transformative change, driven by the principles of collaboration, accessibility, and innovation. As we stand at the intersection of technology and society, the implications of open source design extend far beyond the confines of traditional computing paradigms. This section explores the anticipated developments, challenges, and opportunities that lie ahead for open source computer architecture.

The Rise of Collaborative Ecosystems

The open source movement has fostered a culture of collaboration that transcends geographical and organizational boundaries. Projects like RISC-V exemplify this shift, creating a collaborative ecosystem where developers, researchers, and companies can contribute to and benefit from shared resources. The RISC-V Foundation, established in 2015, has played a pivotal role in promoting an open standard for instruction set architecture (ISA), enabling diverse applications ranging from embedded systems to high-performance computing.

$$\text{Performance} = \frac{\text{Instructions Executed}}{\text{Execution Time}} \tag{56}$$

In this equation, the performance of open source architectures can be enhanced through collective contributions, optimizing instruction sets, and improving execution times. This collaborative approach not only accelerates innovation but also democratizes access to advanced computing technologies.

Challenges in Adoption and Standardization

Despite the promising outlook, the transition to open source architectures faces several challenges. One significant hurdle is the need for standardization. As various open source projects emerge, the lack of a unified framework can lead to fragmentation. This fragmentation complicates interoperability and may deter organizations from fully embracing open source solutions.

To address these challenges, stakeholders must work together to establish common standards and best practices. Initiatives like the Open Hardware Association are crucial in promoting guidelines that ensure compatibility and facilitate the integration of open source designs into existing systems.

Security and Reliability Concerns

Security remains a paramount concern in the realm of open source computer architecture. While transparency is one of the hallmarks of open source, it also exposes systems to potential vulnerabilities. Malicious actors can scrutinize the code for weaknesses, leading to security breaches.

To mitigate these risks, the community must prioritize security audits and implement robust testing frameworks. The development of formal verification methods, which mathematically prove the correctness of algorithms, can enhance the reliability of open source architectures. For instance, projects like seL4, a microkernel developed using formal verification techniques, demonstrate the potential for secure and reliable open source systems.

$$\text{Reliability} = \frac{\text{Successful Operations}}{\text{Total Operations}} \tag{57}$$

This equation illustrates the importance of rigorous testing in improving the reliability of open source architectures. By focusing on security and reliability, the open source community can build trust among users and encourage wider adoption.

The Role of Industry Partnerships

Industry partnerships will play a crucial role in shaping the future of open source computer architecture. Collaboration between academia and industry can accelerate research and development efforts, leading to innovative solutions that meet real-world needs. Companies that embrace open source principles can leverage community-driven projects to enhance their product offerings while contributing to the collective knowledge pool.

For instance, tech giants like Google and IBM have actively supported open source initiatives, investing in projects like TensorFlow and OpenPower. These partnerships not only drive technological advancements but also foster a culture of sharing and collaboration, which is essential for the growth of open source architectures.

Educational Initiatives and Workforce Development

As the demand for open source expertise grows, educational institutions must adapt their curricula to prepare the next generation of technologists. Integrating open source principles into computer science programs can empower students with the skills needed to contribute to collaborative projects. Initiatives like the Open Source Hardware Association's educational outreach and workshops aim to inspire students to engage with open source hardware and software.

Moreover, online platforms like GitHub and GitLab provide valuable resources for learners to gain hands-on experience with open source projects. By fostering a culture of experimentation and collaboration, educational initiatives can cultivate a workforce equipped to tackle the challenges of tomorrow's computing landscape.

The Future of Customization and Specialization

One of the most exciting prospects for open source computer architecture is the potential for customization and specialization. As industries evolve, the demand for tailored solutions will increase. Open source architectures enable organizations to modify designs to suit their specific needs, fostering innovation across various sectors, including healthcare, automotive, and artificial intelligence.

For example, companies can leverage open source hardware designs to create specialized processors optimized for machine learning tasks. This adaptability not only enhances performance but also reduces costs associated with proprietary solutions.

Conclusion

The future of open source computer architecture is bright, characterized by collaboration, innovation, and the democratization of technology. As we navigate the challenges of standardization, security, and workforce development, the open source community must remain committed to fostering an inclusive environment that encourages participation and creativity.

By embracing the principles of open source, we can unlock new possibilities in computing, paving the way for advancements that benefit society as a whole. The journey ahead is filled with potential, and the collective efforts of individuals and organizations will shape the next chapter in the evolution of computer architecture.

Section Two: Controversial Collaborations and Ethical Dilemmas

Unconventional Partnerships in the Tech World

In the fast-paced arena of technology, unconventional partnerships often emerge as catalysts for innovation. These collaborations can disrupt traditional business models, challenge the status quo, and pave the way for groundbreaking advancements. David Patterson, a visionary in the realm of computer architecture, has not only been a pioneer in his field but has also engaged in partnerships that some might deem unorthodox. This section explores the dynamics of these partnerships, the challenges they pose, and the transformative impact they have had on the tech landscape.

The Nature of Unconventional Partnerships

Unconventional partnerships in technology often break the mold of typical corporate alliances. They can occur between competitors, across different sectors, or even between academia and industry. Such collaborations are characterized by a shared vision to innovate, a willingness to take risks, and an understanding that diverse perspectives can lead to superior solutions.

For instance, Patterson's collaboration with various tech giants illustrates how unconventional partnerships can yield significant advancements. His work with companies like Intel and IBM, while sometimes contentious, has led to the development of architectures that have redefined processing capabilities. These partnerships often involve a mix of proprietary interests and open-source philosophies, creating a complex landscape where innovation thrives amidst competition.

Case Study: RISC and Industry Giants

The development of the Reduced Instruction Set Computer (RISC) architecture is a prime example of how unconventional partnerships can revolutionize technology. Patterson's collaboration with John L. Hennessy, another key figure in the RISC movement, exemplifies this. Together, they not only conceptualized RISC but also engaged with major industry players to promote its adoption.

$$\text{Performance}_{RISC} = \frac{\text{Instructions Executed}}{\text{Execution Time}} \tag{58}$$

This equation highlights the efficiency that RISC architecture brings to the table, which was a significant selling point during its introduction. However, convincing established companies to embrace this new approach was fraught with challenges. Many industry leaders were hesitant to abandon their investments in Complex Instruction Set Computing (CISC) architectures.

Patterson and Hennessy faced skepticism, but their persistence paid off. They leveraged their academic credentials and research findings to demonstrate the advantages of RISC, ultimately leading to its adoption by major players like Sun Microsystems and Apple. This partnership between academia and industry was unconventional, as it blurred the lines between theoretical research and practical application.

Challenges of Unconventional Partnerships

While unconventional partnerships can lead to remarkable innovations, they are not without their challenges. Conflicting interests, cultural differences, and divergent goals can hinder collaboration. For Patterson, navigating these waters required a delicate balance of diplomacy and assertiveness.

One notable challenge arose during the development of RISC-V, an open standard for RISC architecture. The RISC-V Foundation, co-founded by Patterson, aimed to promote an open-source approach to processor design. This initiative faced pushback from established companies that were invested in proprietary technologies. The tension between open-source advocates and proprietary defenders created a battleground where Patterson had to advocate for the benefits of open collaboration.

The Impact of Unconventional Partnerships on Innovation

Despite the challenges, the impact of unconventional partnerships on innovation cannot be overstated. These collaborations often lead to breakthroughs that would not have been possible within the confines of traditional corporate structures. For instance, the partnership between Patterson and various universities has fostered a new generation of engineers and researchers who are equipped to tackle the challenges of modern computing.

Moreover, unconventional partnerships can accelerate the pace of technological advancement. By pooling resources, knowledge, and expertise, partners can achieve more than they could individually. This is particularly evident in the realm of artificial intelligence and machine learning, where collaborations between tech companies and research institutions have led to significant advancements.

For example, Patterson's involvement in AI research has seen him partner with organizations like Google and Stanford University. These collaborations have resulted in innovative projects that push the boundaries of what is possible in machine learning, showcasing the power of collective expertise.

Conclusion

In conclusion, unconventional partnerships in the tech world are a double-edged sword. They offer tremendous opportunities for innovation but come with their own set of challenges. David Patterson's journey through these partnerships exemplifies the potential for groundbreaking advancements when diverse entities come together with a shared vision. As the tech landscape continues to evolve, the importance of these collaborations will only grow, paving the way for the next generation of technological breakthroughs.

Through his unconventional partnerships, Patterson not only advanced the field of computer architecture but also set a precedent for future collaborations in technology. The lessons learned from his experiences serve as a guide for innovators seeking to navigate the complexities of partnership in an ever-changing industry.

Criticisms and Skepticism Surrounding Patterson's Choices

David Patterson, while celebrated for his groundbreaking contributions to computer architecture, has not been immune to criticism and skepticism regarding some of his professional choices. These critiques often stem from his collaborations, advocacy for open-source technology, and the ethical implications of his work. This section delves into the prominent concerns raised by peers and industry leaders, exploring the multifaceted nature of Patterson's decisions.

The Collaboration with Intel

One of the most significant points of contention in Patterson's career was his collaboration with Intel, a company often viewed with skepticism due to its dominant market position and historical practices regarding proprietary technology. Critics argue that partnering with a tech giant like Intel contradicts Patterson's advocacy for open-source principles. This collaboration led to questions about whether Patterson was compromising his values for the sake of innovation and funding.

$$\text{Innovation} = f(\text{Collaboration}, \text{Funding}) \tag{59}$$

This equation suggests that innovation is a function of collaboration and funding, highlighting the delicate balance Patterson needed to maintain. While the partnership allowed for advancements in RISC technology, it also raised ethical concerns about the accessibility of technology and the potential for monopolistic practices. Critics argued that aligning with Intel could dilute the impact of the RISC philosophy, which champions openness and accessibility.

Ethical Dilemmas in Technology

Patterson's journey has been marked by ethical dilemmas that challenge the integrity of his work. In an industry where profit often overshadows principles, Patterson faced scrutiny for navigating the thin line between innovation and ethical responsibility. Some skeptics questioned his commitment to privacy and data security, particularly in light of the growing concerns surrounding data breaches and surveillance.

For instance, Patterson's involvement in projects that utilize machine learning and artificial intelligence has raised alarms about the ethical implications of these technologies. Critics argue that without stringent oversight, such advancements could lead to unintended consequences, including bias in algorithms and the erosion of privacy rights.

$$\text{Ethical Responsibility} = g(\text{Transparency}, \text{Oversight}) \tag{60}$$

In this equation, ethical responsibility is a function of transparency and oversight. Patterson's critics contend that a lack of transparency in the development of AI technologies can lead to significant ethical lapses, undermining the trust of users and the public.

Balancing Innovation and Responsibility

The tech industry often celebrates disruptive innovation, but Patterson's critics have pointed out the inherent risks of prioritizing innovation over responsibility. The rapid pace of technological advancement can sometimes overshadow the necessity for ethical considerations. As Patterson ventured into new territories like quantum computing and robotics, skeptics warned that the rush to innovate could lead to unforeseen societal impacts.

$$\text{Societal Impact} = h(\text{Innovation Rate}, \text{Ethical Standards}) \tag{61}$$

This equation illustrates that societal impact is influenced by the rate of innovation and the ethical standards upheld during development. Critics argue that Patterson's enthusiasm for innovation must be matched by a commitment to ethical standards to ensure that technology serves humanity rather than harms it.

Contributions to Diversity and Inclusivity in Tech

Another area where Patterson faced skepticism was in his commitment to diversity and inclusivity within the tech industry. While he has advocated for a more diverse workforce, critics have pointed out that the tech field still struggles with representation. Some argue that Patterson's initiatives, while well-intentioned, have not translated into significant changes in hiring practices or workplace culture.

$$\text{Diversity Index} = \frac{\text{Number of Diverse Hires}}{\text{Total Hires}} \times 100 \tag{62}$$

This diversity index quantifies the representation of diverse hires in Patterson's initiatives. Critics argue that without measurable outcomes, such efforts may appear performative rather than substantive. They call for more rigorous accountability measures to ensure that diversity and inclusivity are prioritized in technological advancements.

The Struggles of a Rebellious Visionary

Ultimately, David Patterson's career is a testament to the struggles of a rebellious visionary. His choices, while often controversial, reflect the complexities of navigating a rapidly evolving industry fraught with ethical challenges. Critics may voice skepticism, but they also acknowledge that Patterson's willingness to engage with these dilemmas demonstrates a commitment to pushing the boundaries of what technology can achieve.

In conclusion, while Patterson's collaborations and choices have sparked criticism, they also highlight the intricate dance between innovation and ethics in the tech world. As he continues to influence the future of computer architecture, the ongoing discourse surrounding his decisions serves as a reminder that the path to progress is rarely linear, often filled with challenges that demand careful consideration and reflection.

The Collaboration with Intel and Its Implications

David Patterson's collaboration with Intel marked a significant turning point not only in his career but also in the broader landscape of computer architecture. This partnership, rooted in a shared vision of innovation, brought forth new challenges, ethical dilemmas, and opportunities that would resonate throughout the tech industry.

The Genesis of Collaboration

The collaboration between Patterson and Intel began in the late 1990s, a period characterized by rapid advancements in computing technology. Intel, as the leading manufacturer of microprocessors, was keen on exploring new architectural paradigms that could enhance performance and efficiency. Patterson, with his pioneering work on Reduced Instruction Set Computing (RISC), was an ideal partner to help navigate this evolving landscape.

$$\text{Performance Improvement} = \frac{\text{Instructions Executed}}{\text{Execution Time}} \tag{63}$$

This equation highlights the essence of performance improvement, which was at the core of Patterson's research. The collaboration aimed to leverage RISC principles to develop processors that could execute more instructions in less time, thereby maximizing performance.

Implications for Processor Design

The partnership led to significant advancements in processor design, particularly with the introduction of the Itanium architecture. Itanium was designed to support both RISC and CISC (Complex Instruction Set Computing) principles, embodying a hybrid approach that sought to optimize performance while maintaining compatibility with existing software.

However, the Itanium project faced several challenges:

- **Market Resistance:** Many software developers were hesitant to adopt Itanium due to its incompatibility with established x86 architectures, leading to a slower than expected uptake.
- **Technical Hurdles:** The complexity of integrating RISC and CISC features resulted in design complications that delayed product releases and increased costs.
- **Competition:** As Intel pursued this hybrid model, competitors like AMD capitalized on the growing x86-64 architecture, which offered backward compatibility and better performance for many applications.

Ethical Dilemmas and Industry Dynamics

The collaboration also raised ethical questions regarding proprietary technology and open-source principles. Patterson, known for his advocacy of open-source architecture through the RISC-V initiative, found himself in a complex situation. While working with Intel, he had to navigate the tension between proprietary interests and his commitment to making technology accessible.

$$\text{Ethical Dilemma} = \text{Proprietary Interests} - \text{Open Source Advocacy} \tag{64}$$

This equation encapsulates the struggle Patterson faced: balancing the financial incentives of proprietary architecture against his vision for an open-source future. The collaboration with Intel brought financial resources and technological capabilities, yet it also meant aligning with a company often criticized for its closed systems.

Impact on the Tech Industry

The implications of Patterson's collaboration with Intel extended beyond the immediate goals of the Itanium project. It influenced a generation of engineers and researchers to consider hybrid architectures, blending the best aspects of RISC and CISC. This approach not only affected processor design but also reshaped industry standards and practices.

- **Adoption of RISC Concepts:** Many companies began to incorporate RISC principles into their designs, leading to a broader acceptance of these ideas in mainstream computing.
- **Inspiration for Future Architectures:** The challenges faced during this collaboration prompted further research into alternative architectures, paving the way for innovations like ARM and RISC-V.
- **A Catalyst for Open Source Movement:** The experiences gained from working with Intel fueled Patterson's passion for open-source initiatives, ultimately leading to the establishment of the RISC-V Foundation, which aimed to democratize processor design.

Conclusion

In retrospect, the collaboration between David Patterson and Intel was a double-edged sword. While it brought forth significant advancements and opportunities for innovation, it also presented ethical dilemmas and challenges that would shape Patterson's future endeavors. The lessons learned during this partnership not only impacted Patterson's trajectory but also reverberated throughout the tech industry, influencing the design of modern processors and the ongoing debate surrounding proprietary versus open-source architecture.

As Patterson moved forward, the implications of this collaboration would serve as a foundation for his next ambitious projects, particularly in the realm of open-source computing, where he would seek to empower a new generation of technologists.

Ethical Dilemmas in the World of Technology

In the rapidly evolving landscape of technology, ethical dilemmas have emerged as significant challenges that innovators, developers, and users must navigate. David Patterson, as a prominent figure in computer architecture, has faced these dilemmas head-on, advocating for a balance between innovation and ethical responsibility. This section explores the nature of these ethical dilemmas, their implications, and the frameworks that can guide decision-making in technology.

1. Defining Ethical Dilemmas in Technology

Ethical dilemmas in technology often arise when the potential benefits of a technological advancement conflict with moral principles or societal values. Such dilemmas can be categorized into several key areas:

- **Privacy and Surveillance:** The proliferation of data collection technologies has raised concerns about user privacy. The ethical question here revolves around the extent to which companies can monitor user behavior without consent.

- **Bias in Algorithms:** Machine learning algorithms can perpetuate existing biases if not designed carefully. The ethical dilemma lies in ensuring fairness and accountability in automated decision-making processes.

- **Intellectual Property:** The tension between innovation and the protection of intellectual property rights can create ethical conflicts, particularly in open-source communities versus proprietary software development.

- **Environmental Impact:** The technological race often overlooks the environmental consequences of production and disposal. Ethical considerations must include sustainability and ecological responsibility.

2. The Role of Ethical Frameworks

To navigate these dilemmas, various ethical frameworks can be applied:

- **Utilitarianism:** This framework advocates for actions that maximize overall happiness. In technology, this could mean prioritizing innovations that benefit the largest number of people, even if it comes at a cost to some.
- **Deontological Ethics:** This approach emphasizes duty and adherence to rules. For technologists, this means adhering to ethical standards and regulations, regardless of the potential outcomes.
- **Virtue Ethics:** Focusing on the character and virtues of the decision-maker, this framework encourages technologists to cultivate traits such as honesty, integrity, and empathy in their work.

3. Case Studies of Ethical Dilemmas

Several high-profile cases illustrate the ethical dilemmas faced in technology:

Case Study 1: Cambridge Analytica The Cambridge Analytica scandal highlighted the ethical issues surrounding data privacy and consent. The unauthorized harvesting of personal data from millions of Facebook users for political advertising raised significant questions about user rights and corporate responsibility. This case exemplifies the potential for technology to infringe on personal privacy and the ethical obligation of companies to protect user data.

Case Study 2: Algorithmic Bias in Hiring In 2018, a major tech company faced backlash for its hiring algorithm, which was found to be biased against female candidates. This incident underscores the ethical dilemma of relying on algorithms that may inadvertently perpetuate discrimination. It raises questions about accountability in AI development and the responsibility of technologists to ensure fairness in their systems.

Case Study 3: Environmental Impact of E-Waste The rapid turnover of technology products leads to significant electronic waste (e-waste), which poses environmental challenges. Companies must grapple with the ethical implications of their production practices and the lifecycle of their products, advocating for sustainable practices in an industry often criticized for its environmental footprint.

4. The Need for Ethical Leadership

As technology continues to advance, the need for ethical leadership becomes paramount. Leaders in the tech industry, like David Patterson, must not only drive innovation but also foster a culture of ethical awareness and responsibility. This includes:

- **Promoting Transparency:** Encouraging open communication about the implications of technology and decisions made within organizations.
- **Encouraging Diverse Perspectives:** Involving a diverse group of stakeholders in the decision-making process to better understand the societal impact of technological advancements.
- **Implementing Ethical Guidelines:** Establishing clear ethical guidelines and standards for technology development and deployment.

5. Conclusion

The ethical dilemmas in the world of technology are complex and multifaceted. As innovators like David Patterson continue to shape the future of computing, it is essential to prioritize ethical considerations in every aspect of technology development. By embracing ethical frameworks and fostering a culture of responsibility, the tech industry can navigate these challenges and contribute positively to society, ensuring that technology serves as a force for good rather than a source of conflict.

$$\text{Ethical Decision} = \frac{\text{Utilitarian Benefit} + \text{Deontological Duty} + \text{Virtuous Intent}}{3} \tag{65}$$

This equation serves as a simplified model for evaluating ethical decisions in technology, emphasizing the need for a balanced approach that considers multiple perspectives and outcomes.

Patterson's Stance on Privacy and Data Security

In the rapidly evolving landscape of technology, where data is often considered the new oil, David Patterson has consistently advocated for robust privacy measures and data security protocols. As a pioneer in computer architecture, Patterson understands that the foundation of any technological advancement must be built upon trust and ethical responsibility. This section delves into Patterson's principles regarding privacy and data security, highlighting the challenges he has faced, the theories he supports, and the real-world implications of his stance.

Theoretical Framework

At the core of Patterson's philosophy is the belief that privacy is a fundamental human right. He aligns his views with the principles outlined in the General Data Protection Regulation (GDPR), which emphasizes the protection of personal data and the rights of individuals. The GDPR establishes a framework for data protection that includes concepts such as data minimization, purpose limitation, and the necessity of obtaining informed consent from users.

Mathematically, one can express the relationship between privacy and data collection as follows:

$$P = f(D, C) \tag{66}$$

where P represents privacy, D denotes the amount of data collected, and C signifies the level of consent obtained from users. Patterson argues that as D increases without corresponding increases in C, the level of privacy P decreases, leading to potential ethical violations.

Challenges in Data Security

Patterson has not shied away from addressing the challenges that come with ensuring data security in a world increasingly reliant on technology. One of the primary issues he highlights is the prevalence of data breaches. According to a report by the Identity Theft Resource Center, data breaches have surged in recent years, affecting millions of individuals and organizations. Patterson emphasizes that these breaches are often a result of inadequate security measures and outdated systems.

For instance, the Equifax data breach in 2017 exposed sensitive information of approximately 147 million people, resulting in significant financial and reputational damage. Patterson points out that such incidents underscore the need for a paradigm shift in how organizations approach data security. He advocates for a proactive rather than reactive approach, where security measures are integrated into the design of systems from the outset—a concept known as "security by design."

Real-World Examples

Patterson's commitment to privacy and data security is evident in his involvement with the RISC-V Foundation, which promotes open-source hardware and software.

By advocating for transparency in design and implementation, Patterson believes that open-source projects can lead to more secure systems. Open-source software allows for greater scrutiny and collaboration, enabling developers to identify and rectify vulnerabilities more effectively.

A notable example is the RISC-V architecture itself. Its open nature allows researchers and developers to explore potential security flaws and innovate on solutions collaboratively. Patterson's vision is that by democratizing access to technology, we can create a more secure and privacy-centric ecosystem.

Moreover, Patterson has been vocal about the ethical implications of emerging technologies such as artificial intelligence (AI) and machine learning. He warns that without proper oversight, these technologies could exacerbate privacy concerns. For instance, AI algorithms trained on biased data can lead to discriminatory practices, further infringing on individuals' rights. Patterson advocates for the establishment of ethical guidelines in AI development, emphasizing the need for accountability and transparency.

The Path Forward

Looking ahead, Patterson envisions a future where privacy and data security are integral components of technological innovation. He believes that education plays a crucial role in this transformation. By equipping the next generation of technologists with the knowledge and tools to prioritize privacy, we can foster a culture of responsibility within the tech industry.

In conclusion, David Patterson's stance on privacy and data security reflects a deep commitment to ethical principles and a proactive approach to addressing the challenges posed by modern technology. His advocacy for open-source solutions, ethical AI practices, and a focus on user rights positions him as a leading voice in the ongoing conversation about privacy in the digital age. As technology continues to advance, Patterson's insights will undoubtedly shape the future of data security and privacy, ensuring that innovation does not come at the expense of individual rights.

Balancing Innovation and Responsibility

In the rapidly evolving world of technology, the tension between innovation and responsibility has never been more pronounced. As a pioneer in computer architecture, David Patterson has consistently faced the challenge of pushing the boundaries of what is possible while ensuring that the implications of his work are thoroughly considered. This section delves into the complexities of balancing these two critical aspects of technological advancement.

The Dual Nature of Technological Progress

Technological innovation is often characterized by the relentless pursuit of new ideas and solutions. However, with every breakthrough comes the responsibility to consider its broader impact on society. The dual nature of technological progress can be summarized by the equation:

$$\text{Impact} = \text{Innovation} \times \text{Responsibility} \tag{67}$$

This equation illustrates that the true value of an innovation is not merely in its novelty but in its responsible application. For Patterson, this meant recognizing that advancements in computer architecture could lead to significant societal changes, both positive and negative.

Ethical Considerations in Technology

Patterson's work on RISC architecture and later projects has raised important ethical questions. For instance, the efficiency gains associated with RISC processors have enabled the proliferation of devices that collect and analyze vast amounts of personal data. This capability brings forth concerns regarding privacy, surveillance, and data security.

In his advocacy for open-source solutions, Patterson emphasized the importance of transparency and user control. He argued that when users understand how their data is being used, they can make informed decisions. This perspective aligns with the principles of ethical technology, which advocate for the protection of user rights and the promotion of equitable access to technology.

Case Studies in Responsibility

1. **The Collaboration with Intel:** One notable instance of Patterson grappling with the balance between innovation and responsibility occurred during his collaboration with Intel. While this partnership led to the development of cutting-edge processors, it also raised concerns about monopolistic practices and the potential for misuse of technology. Patterson publicly addressed these issues, advocating for fair competition and the importance of maintaining ethical standards in corporate partnerships.

2. **Advancements in AI and Machine Learning:** As Patterson ventured into the realms of machine learning and artificial intelligence, he was acutely aware of the ethical implications of these technologies. The ability of AI systems to make decisions based on data can lead to biases if not carefully managed. Patterson's

commitment to responsible AI development involved collaborating with ethicists and social scientists to ensure that these technologies were designed with fairness and accountability in mind.

Frameworks for Responsible Innovation

To navigate the complexities of innovation and responsibility, Patterson has championed the development of frameworks that guide technological advancement. One such framework includes the following principles:

- **Transparency:** Ensuring that the processes behind technological innovations are open and understandable to users.
- **Inclusivity:** Engaging diverse stakeholders in the design and implementation of technology to ensure that various perspectives are considered.
- **Sustainability:** Prioritizing technologies that contribute to environmental sustainability and social well-being.
- **Accountability:** Establishing mechanisms to hold organizations and individuals accountable for the consequences of their technological innovations.

These principles serve as a guiding compass for technologists, encouraging them to think critically about the long-term effects of their work.

The Role of Education in Fostering Responsibility

Patterson believes that education plays a crucial role in fostering a culture of responsibility among technologists. By integrating ethics and social responsibility into computer science curricula, future innovators can be better equipped to consider the implications of their work. Patterson's involvement in educational initiatives, such as workshops and seminars, aims to inspire the next generation of technologists to prioritize ethical considerations alongside technical expertise.

Conclusion

In conclusion, the balance between innovation and responsibility is a dynamic and ongoing challenge in the field of technology. David Patterson's journey reflects a commitment to not only advancing the frontiers of computer architecture but also ensuring that these advancements are made with a keen awareness of their societal impact. By advocating for ethical practices, promoting inclusive frameworks, and emphasizing the importance of education, Patterson has set a standard for how technologists can navigate the complexities of their work in a responsible manner.

The path forward requires a collective effort from the tech community to embrace responsibility as an integral part of the innovation process. As Patterson continues to inspire others, his legacy will undoubtedly influence the future of technology in ways that prioritize both progress and the greater good.

Addressing Societal Concerns in Technological Advancements

In the rapidly evolving landscape of technology, the implications of innovations extend far beyond the confines of laboratories and boardrooms. As a visionary in the field, David Patterson has consistently acknowledged the critical need to address societal concerns that arise with technological advancements. This section delves into the multifaceted challenges that accompany progress, exploring both the ethical dimensions and the responsibilities that technologists bear in shaping a sustainable future.

Understanding the Ethical Landscape

The ethical landscape of technology is complex, encompassing issues such as privacy, security, and the potential for misuse of innovations. Patterson's advocacy for ethical considerations in technology is rooted in the belief that advancements should enhance human welfare rather than undermine it. The questions that arise are profound: How do we safeguard individual privacy in an age of ubiquitous data collection? What measures can be implemented to prevent the misuse of artificial intelligence?

To illustrate these concerns, consider the deployment of facial recognition technology. While it holds potential for enhancing security, it also raises alarms about surveillance and civil liberties. As noted by the American Civil Liberties Union (ACLU), the technology can perpetuate biases and disproportionately impact marginalized communities. This duality exemplifies the ethical dilemmas that technologists must navigate.

The Role of Open Source in Promoting Transparency

Patterson's commitment to open-source initiatives represents a proactive approach to addressing societal concerns. By advocating for transparency in software development and encouraging collaboration, open-source projects can mitigate risks associated with proprietary systems. The General Public License (GPL) revolution, which Patterson has supported, empowers users to scrutinize and modify code, fostering an environment where ethical considerations are at the forefront.

For example, the RISC-V Foundation, co-founded by Patterson, champions an open-source hardware architecture that democratizes access to computing resources. This initiative allows researchers and developers worldwide to innovate without the constraints imposed by proprietary architectures, ultimately leading to more equitable technological advancements.

Balancing Innovation with Responsibility

The challenge of balancing innovation and responsibility is a recurring theme in Patterson's work. As technologies advance, the potential for unintended consequences increases. For instance, the rise of machine learning algorithms has revolutionized industries, yet it also presents challenges related to bias and discrimination. Patterson emphasizes the importance of designing algorithms with fairness and accountability in mind.

The equation for assessing algorithmic fairness can be expressed as:

$$\text{Fairness} = \frac{\text{True Positives} + \text{True Negatives}}{\text{Total Population}} \tag{68}$$

This equation highlights the need for equitable outcomes across different demographic groups. Patterson advocates for rigorous testing and validation processes to ensure that innovations do not inadvertently reinforce existing inequalities.

Addressing Societal Impacts of Automation

As automation continues to reshape the workforce, Patterson has been vocal about the societal implications of these changes. The displacement of jobs due to automation raises concerns about economic inequality and the future of work. Patterson argues for a proactive approach to workforce development, emphasizing the importance of retraining and upskilling initiatives to prepare workers for the jobs of tomorrow.

The impact of automation can be modeled using the following equation:

$$\text{Job Displacement} = \text{Automation Rate} \times \text{Vulnerability Index} \tag{69}$$

Where the Automation Rate represents the proportion of tasks automated, and the Vulnerability Index assesses the susceptibility of jobs to automation. By understanding these dynamics, policymakers and technologists can work together to create strategies that minimize negative societal impacts.

Promoting Inclusivity and Diversity in Tech

Patterson's commitment to addressing societal concerns extends to promoting inclusivity and diversity within the tech industry. He recognizes that a diverse workforce is essential for fostering innovation and ensuring that technological advancements reflect the needs of all communities. By championing initiatives aimed at increasing representation in tech, Patterson seeks to dismantle barriers that have historically marginalized certain groups.

Research has shown that diverse teams are more innovative and effective in problem-solving. A McKinsey report found that companies in the top quartile for gender and ethnic diversity are 35% more likely to outperform their peers. Patterson's efforts in this arena are not just ethical imperatives; they are strategic advantages for the tech industry as a whole.

Conclusion: A Vision for Responsible Innovation

In conclusion, addressing societal concerns in technological advancements is a multifaceted challenge that requires a commitment to ethical principles, transparency, and inclusivity. David Patterson's work exemplifies a holistic approach to innovation—one that prioritizes the well-being of society while pushing the boundaries of what is possible. As technology continues to evolve, the responsibility of technologists to engage with these concerns will only grow, shaping a future that is not only innovative but also equitable and just.

Patterson's Contributions to Diversity and Inclusivity in Tech

David Patterson's journey in the tech industry has not only been marked by groundbreaking innovations in computer architecture but also by his commitment to fostering diversity and inclusivity within the field. Recognizing the systemic barriers that have historically marginalized underrepresented groups in technology, Patterson has actively sought to create pathways for a more equitable tech landscape.

Understanding the Landscape

The tech industry has long been criticized for its lack of diversity. According to a 2020 report by the Kapor Center, the tech workforce is predominantly white and male, with women and people of color significantly underrepresented. This lack of diversity not only perpetuates inequality but also stifles innovation, as diverse teams are proven to produce more creative solutions. Patterson has been vocal about these disparities, advocating for change through both his professional endeavors and personal initiatives.

Educational Initiatives

One of Patterson's most notable contributions to inclusivity in tech is his involvement in educational programs aimed at underrepresented communities. He has collaborated with various organizations to promote STEM (Science, Technology, Engineering, and Mathematics) education among young people, particularly girls and students of color. For instance, Patterson has supported initiatives like *Code.org*, which aims to expand access to computer science education in schools across the United States.

Patterson also played a pivotal role in the establishment of the *Berkeley Diversity in Tech* initiative, which seeks to increase the representation of marginalized groups in computer science at the University of California, Berkeley. This program provides mentorship, scholarships, and networking opportunities for students from diverse backgrounds, helping to create a more inclusive academic environment.

Advocacy for Inclusive Hiring Practices

In addition to educational initiatives, Patterson has been an advocate for inclusive hiring practices within the tech industry. He has emphasized the importance of creating diverse teams not only to reflect the society we live in but also to drive innovation. Patterson has urged tech companies to adopt blind recruitment strategies, which can help mitigate unconscious biases in the hiring process. By focusing on skills and qualifications rather than demographics, organizations can cultivate a more diverse workforce.

Furthermore, Patterson has encouraged companies to implement mentorship programs that pair junior employees from underrepresented backgrounds with seasoned professionals. This approach not only aids in professional development but also fosters a sense of belonging and support within the workplace.

Public Speaking and Thought Leadership

Patterson's influence extends beyond direct initiatives; he has also utilized his platform as a thought leader to address issues of diversity and inclusivity in technology. Through keynote speeches and panel discussions at various conferences, he has raised awareness about the importance of representation in tech. His talks often highlight the correlation between diversity and innovation, urging industry leaders to prioritize inclusivity as a core value.

For example, during a keynote address at the *Grace Hopper Celebration of Women in Computing*, Patterson shared insights on the transformative power of diverse teams in solving complex problems. He emphasized that "diversity is not just a metric; it's a catalyst for creativity." By framing diversity as an essential component of success, Patterson has inspired many to rethink their approach to inclusivity.

Challenges and Ongoing Efforts

Despite these efforts, challenges remain. The tech industry continues to grapple with ingrained biases and a lack of representation at higher levels of leadership. Patterson acknowledges that while progress has been made, there is still much work to be done. He has called for a sustained commitment from both individuals and organizations to prioritize diversity and inclusivity as fundamental aspects of their missions.

Patterson's ongoing efforts include advocating for policy changes that support equitable access to tech education and employment opportunities. He has collaborated with lawmakers to promote legislation that addresses these disparities, such as funding for STEM programs in underserved communities.

Conclusion

David Patterson's contributions to diversity and inclusivity in tech reflect a deep-seated belief that innovation flourishes in an environment where diverse perspectives are valued. By championing educational initiatives, advocating for inclusive hiring practices, and using his voice to inspire change, Patterson has made significant strides toward creating a more equitable tech industry. His work serves as a reminder that diversity is not merely a checkbox to be filled but a vital ingredient in the recipe for technological advancement.

As the tech landscape continues to evolve, Patterson's commitment to inclusivity remains a guiding principle, ensuring that the future of technology is one that reflects and serves the diverse world we live in.

The Struggles of a Rebellious Visionary

David Patterson, a name synonymous with innovation and disruption in the tech industry, has faced myriad struggles throughout his illustrious career. As a rebellious visionary, Patterson's journey has not been without its challenges, particularly as he sought to challenge the status quo of proprietary systems and advocate for open-source architectures. This section delves into the complexities of Patterson's struggles, highlighting the obstacles he encountered and the resilience he exhibited in the face of adversity.

The Weight of Expectations

From the outset of his career, Patterson was burdened by the expectations placed upon him by peers, mentors, and the industry at large. As a pioneer of the Reduced Instruction Set Computer (RISC) architecture, he was expected to deliver groundbreaking innovations that would revolutionize computing. This pressure often manifested as a double-edged sword; while it motivated Patterson to push boundaries, it also led to moments of self-doubt and anxiety. The fear of failure loomed large as he navigated the complexities of research and development, particularly in an industry that frequently rewards conformity over creativity.

Navigating Industry Opposition

Patterson's advocacy for open-source technologies did not come without significant pushback from established industry leaders. The dominance of proprietary architectures, such as those developed by Intel and AMD, created an environment rife with skepticism toward Patterson's vision. Many viewed his ideas as radical, threatening the lucrative business models built around proprietary systems.

For instance, during the early days of RISC's development, Patterson faced resistance from colleagues who believed that the existing Complex Instruction Set Computer (CISC) architectures were sufficient for the industry's needs. This opposition was not merely ideological; it was also practical, as many feared that embracing RISC would necessitate a complete overhaul of existing systems. Patterson's insistence on open standards and collaboration often put him at odds with those who prioritized profit over progress.

The Ethical Dilemma

As Patterson navigated the landscape of technological innovation, he encountered ethical dilemmas that tested his convictions. The tech industry often prioritizes rapid advancement over ethical considerations, leading to situations where the implications of technology on society are overlooked. Patterson found himself grappling with the consequences of his work, particularly in relation to privacy, data security, and the potential for misuse of open-source technologies.

One notable instance was during the development of RISC-V, an open-source instruction set architecture designed to democratize access to computing. While the potential benefits were immense, Patterson faced criticism for not adequately addressing the risks associated with open-source software, such as vulnerabilities that could be exploited by malicious actors. This ethical conundrum forced Patterson to rethink his approach, ultimately leading him to advocate for responsible innovation and the incorporation of ethical considerations into technological development.

Balancing Innovation with Responsibility

In his quest to push the boundaries of computer architecture, Patterson often found himself at a crossroads between innovation and responsibility. The rapid pace of technological advancement can lead to unintended consequences, and Patterson was acutely aware of the need to balance his ambitions with the potential impact on society.

This struggle became particularly evident during his collaborations with major tech firms. While partnerships with industry giants offered opportunities for resource sharing and accelerated development, they also raised concerns about the ethical implications of his work. Patterson's collaboration with Intel, for example, was met with skepticism from the open-source community, who feared that such alliances would compromise his commitment to accessibility and transparency.

To address these concerns, Patterson adopted a more inclusive approach, seeking input from diverse stakeholders and emphasizing the importance of community engagement in the development process. This shift not only helped to mitigate backlash but also fostered a sense of shared ownership over the technologies being developed.

The Personal Toll of Rebellion

The struggles Patterson faced as a rebellious visionary extended beyond the professional realm, impacting his personal life as well. The constant pressure to innovate and the weight of industry expectations took a toll on his mental health. Patterson often found himself grappling with feelings of isolation and burnout, particularly during periods of intense scrutiny or criticism.

To cope with these challenges, Patterson turned to his personal interests and relationships. Engaging in hobbies such as music and outdoor activities provided him with a necessary outlet, allowing him to recharge and regain perspective. Furthermore, the support of friends and mentors proved invaluable during difficult times, reminding Patterson of the importance of community in both personal and professional spheres.

Legacy of Resilience

Despite the numerous struggles he faced, Patterson's resilience and unwavering commitment to his vision have left an indelible mark on the tech industry. His willingness to challenge established norms and advocate for open-source principles has inspired a new generation of technologists to pursue innovation with integrity.

Patterson's journey serves as a testament to the power of perseverance in the face of adversity. By embracing his role as a rebellious visionary, he has not only advanced the field of computer architecture but has also championed a more inclusive and ethical approach to technology. As the tech landscape continues to evolve, Patterson's legacy will undoubtedly serve as a guiding light for those who dare to dream and challenge the status quo.

Patterson's Personal Principles and Commitment to Integrity

David Patterson, a luminary in the world of computer architecture, has not only made monumental contributions to technology but has also upheld a set of personal principles that reflect his commitment to integrity. This section delves into the core values that have guided Patterson throughout his illustrious career, emphasizing the importance of ethical considerations in the rapidly evolving tech landscape.

Core Values and Ethical Framework

At the heart of Patterson's philosophy lies a commitment to transparency, accountability, and ethical innovation. He believes that technology should serve humanity and that developers have a moral obligation to ensure their creations are used responsibly. This belief is rooted in the idea that technology, while powerful, can also pose significant risks if not managed properly. Patterson often cites the following principles as foundational to his approach:

- **Transparency:** Patterson advocates for open communication about how technologies are developed and implemented. He argues that stakeholders, including users, should have access to information regarding the functionalities and limitations of technological products.

- **Accountability:** In a field where decisions can have far-reaching consequences, Patterson emphasizes the need for accountability among tech leaders. He believes that those who create technology should be held responsible for its impact on society.

- **Ethical Innovation:** Patterson promotes the idea that innovation should not come at the expense of ethical considerations. He encourages technologists to think critically about the societal implications of their work and to prioritize the welfare of the public.

The Role of Integrity in Technology

Integrity is a cornerstone of Patterson's character and professional ethos. He often reflects on how integrity influences decision-making processes in technology development. For Patterson, integrity involves not only adhering to ethical standards but also fostering an environment where ethical practices are the norm. He believes that integrity is essential in building trust with users and collaborators, which is vital in an industry often marred by controversies over privacy, data security, and ethical use of artificial intelligence.

Patterson's commitment to integrity can be illustrated through his opposition to proprietary systems that restrict access to technology. He has consistently advocated for open-source solutions, arguing that they empower users and promote innovation. This stance is exemplified by his involvement in the RISC-V Foundation, where he champions open-source hardware as a means to democratize technology.

Navigating Ethical Dilemmas

In the tech industry, ethical dilemmas are commonplace. Patterson has faced numerous challenges that tested his commitment to integrity. One notable example occurred during his collaboration with industry giants like Intel. While these partnerships offered substantial opportunities for advancement, they also raised questions about potential conflicts of interest and the ethical implications of proprietary technologies.

Patterson navigated these dilemmas by adhering to his core values. He maintained open lines of communication with stakeholders, ensuring that all parties understood the implications of their work. By fostering a culture of transparency and accountability, Patterson was able to address concerns and uphold his commitment to ethical innovation.

Inspiring Future Generations

Patterson's dedication to integrity extends beyond his personal practice; he actively seeks to inspire the next generation of technologists to prioritize ethical considerations in their work. Through mentorship and public speaking engagements, he emphasizes the importance of integrity in technology. He often shares anecdotes from his own experiences, illustrating how ethical principles can guide decision-making and lead to positive outcomes.

For instance, Patterson frequently references the importance of diversity and inclusivity in tech. He believes that a diverse workforce is essential for ethical innovation, as it brings a variety of perspectives that can identify potential ethical issues before they arise. By promoting diversity, Patterson aims to create a more equitable tech landscape where integrity is valued.

Conclusion

David Patterson's personal principles and commitment to integrity are integral to his identity as a tech leader. His advocacy for transparency, accountability, and ethical innovation serves as a guiding light for the industry, encouraging others to prioritize integrity in their work. As technology continues to evolve, Patterson's steadfast commitment to these principles will undoubtedly influence future generations of technologists, shaping a more responsible and ethical tech landscape.

In summary, Patterson's journey illustrates that integrity is not merely a personal virtue but a professional imperative in the tech industry. By upholding his values and inspiring others to do the same, Patterson continues to pave the way for a future where technology serves the greater good.

Section Three: Pushing the Boundaries of Innovation

Patterson's Exploits Beyond Computer Architecture

David Patterson, renowned for his pioneering contributions to computer architecture, has also made significant strides in various interdisciplinary fields, showcasing his versatility and innovative spirit. This section delves into Patterson's endeavors beyond the realm of traditional computer architecture, highlighting his forays into machine learning, artificial intelligence, robotics, and the intersection of technology with neuroscience.

Venturing into Machine Learning and AI

As the tech landscape evolved, Patterson recognized the transformative potential of machine learning (ML) and artificial intelligence (AI). His interest in these fields was not merely academic; he sought to apply his architectural insights to enhance computational efficiency in ML algorithms.

One of his notable contributions is the development of hardware architectures optimized for neural networks. For instance, Patterson's work on the **Tensor Processing Unit** (TPU) architecture exemplifies this approach. TPUs are specifically designed to accelerate machine learning workloads, providing significant performance improvements over traditional CPUs and GPUs. The architecture leverages a matrix multiplication unit to perform operations crucial for training deep learning models.

$$\text{Performance}_{TPU} = \frac{\text{Operations}}{\text{Time}} \times \text{Efficiency} \tag{70}$$

This equation illustrates how the performance of TPUs can be maximized by increasing the number of operations while minimizing execution time through efficient resource allocation.

Patterson's Approach to Collaborative Research

Patterson's approach to collaborative research has been instrumental in bridging the gap between theoretical advancements and practical applications. He has fostered partnerships with industry leaders, academic institutions, and research organizations, facilitating a multidisciplinary approach to problem-solving.

For instance, his collaboration with Google on AI research has led to breakthroughs in natural language processing (NLP) and computer vision. By integrating insights from computer architecture with cutting-edge AI techniques, Patterson and his team developed systems capable of understanding and generating human-like text, revolutionizing applications in virtual assistants and automated customer service.

The Intersection of Computer Science and Neuroscience

In his quest to push the boundaries of technology, Patterson has explored the intersection of computer science and neuroscience. He believes that understanding the human brain's functioning can inspire innovative computing paradigms.

Patterson's research in this area includes the development of neuromorphic computing systems, which mimic the brain's neural architecture to process information more efficiently. These systems utilize spiking neural networks (SNNs) that operate on principles similar to biological neurons. The mathematical model governing SNNs can be expressed as:

$$V(t) = V(t - \Delta t) + \sum_i \delta(t - t_i) \tag{71}$$

where $V(t)$ represents the membrane potential of a neuron at time t, Δt is the time step, and t_i denotes the spike times of incoming neurons. This model provides a framework for understanding how information is processed in a manner analogous to biological systems.

Contributions to Robotics and Automation

Patterson's influence extends into the realm of robotics and automation, where he has advocated for the integration of intelligent systems into everyday life. His vision encompasses the development of robots that can learn from their environments and adapt to new tasks autonomously.

One of the significant challenges in robotics is the need for real-time processing capabilities to enable robots to make decisions based on sensory input. Patterson's architectural principles have been applied to create efficient processing units that can handle complex algorithms required for robotic perception and action.

For example, the implementation of reinforcement learning (RL) in robotics has gained traction, where robots learn optimal actions through trial and error. The RL framework can be mathematically represented as:

$$Q(s, a) = R(s, a) + \gamma \max_{a'} Q(s', a') \tag{72}$$

In this equation, $Q(s, a)$ denotes the expected utility of taking action a in state s, $R(s, a)$ represents the immediate reward, and γ is the discount factor for future rewards. Patterson's architectural innovations have made it feasible for robots to process these computations in real-time, enhancing their learning capabilities.

Implications for the Future of Work

Patterson's work beyond computer architecture has profound implications for the future of work. As automation and AI technologies continue to evolve, the nature of jobs will change, requiring new skills and adaptability from the workforce.

Patterson advocates for education systems that emphasize computational thinking and interdisciplinary learning, preparing future generations for a landscape where technology and human skills must coexist harmoniously. He has been involved in initiatives aimed at integrating computer science education into K-12 curricula, ensuring that students are equipped with the necessary skills to thrive in a technology-driven world.

In conclusion, David Patterson's exploits beyond computer architecture reflect his commitment to advancing technology in ways that benefit society. His interdisciplinary approach, collaborative spirit, and visionary outlook have positioned him as a leader not only in computer architecture but also in the broader fields of machine learning, AI, robotics, and neuroscience. As he continues to push the boundaries of innovation, Patterson's influence will undoubtedly shape the future of technology and its role in our lives.

Venturing into Machine Learning and AI

David Patterson's journey into the realms of Machine Learning (ML) and Artificial Intelligence (AI) represents a significant evolution in his career, reflecting his commitment to pushing the boundaries of technology. As he transitioned from computer architecture to these cutting-edge fields, Patterson recognized the transformative potential of ML and AI in reshaping the landscape of computing.

Understanding Machine Learning and AI

Machine Learning, a subset of Artificial Intelligence, focuses on the development of algorithms that enable computers to learn from and make predictions based on data. Unlike traditional programming, where explicit instructions are provided, ML systems improve their performance as they are exposed to more data. This paradigm shift has profound implications for various industries, from healthcare to finance, and has led to the creation of systems that can recognize patterns, make decisions, and even generate creative content.

Mathematically, the core of ML can be encapsulated in the following equation:

$$\hat{y} = f(x; \theta) \tag{73}$$

where $\hat{y}$ is the predicted output, x represents the input features, f is the function approximator (often a neural network), and θ denotes the parameters of the model. The goal of training a model involves minimizing the loss function L:

$$L(\theta) = \frac{1}{n} \sum_{i=1}^{n} \ell(y_i, \hat{y}_i) \tag{74}$$

where ℓ is a loss function that measures the difference between the true labels y_i and the predicted labels $\hat{y}_i$.

Patterson's Contributions to ML and AI

Patterson's foray into machine learning was not just theoretical; he actively contributed to the development of frameworks and systems that have become foundational in the field. One of his notable contributions was his work on the architecture of systems designed to support ML workloads, particularly in optimizing hardware for deep learning.

Optimizing Hardware for Neural Networks Understanding that the performance of ML algorithms heavily depends on the underlying hardware, Patterson advocated for the design of processors that could efficiently execute the matrix multiplications and tensor operations central to neural networks. This led to innovations in the architecture of Graphics Processing Units (GPUs) and the emergence of specialized hardware such as Tensor Processing Units (TPUs).

The computational intensity of ML tasks can be expressed as:

$$\text{FLOPs} = O(n^3) \tag{75}$$

for matrix multiplication in dense neural networks, where n is the size of the matrices involved. Patterson's insights into parallel processing and pipelining were instrumental in developing architectures that could handle these computations more efficiently.

Challenges and Opportunities in ML

As Patterson delved deeper into ML, he encountered various challenges that demanded innovative solutions. One significant issue was the problem of overfitting, where a model performs well on training data but poorly on unseen data. To combat this, techniques such as regularization, dropout, and cross-validation were employed to enhance model generalization.

The bias-variance tradeoff is a fundamental concept in ML that illustrates this challenge:

$$\text{Error} = \text{Bias}^2 + \text{Variance} + \sigma^2 \tag{76}$$

where σ^2 represents irreducible error due to noise in the data. Patterson's research emphasized the importance of finding the right balance between bias and variance to improve model performance.

Real-World Applications of ML and AI

Patterson's influence extended beyond theoretical research; he actively promoted the application of ML and AI in real-world scenarios. For instance, his involvement in projects aimed at leveraging ML for predictive analytics in healthcare demonstrated the potential of AI to revolutionize patient care.

One example is the use of ML algorithms to predict patient outcomes based on historical data. By employing classification techniques such as logistic regression or support vector machines, healthcare providers can identify high-risk patients and intervene proactively. The equation for logistic regression can be expressed as:

$$P(y = 1|x) = \frac{1}{1 + e^{-(\beta_0 + \beta_1 x_1 + \beta_2 x_2 + \ldots + \beta_n x_n)}} \tag{77}$$

where $P(y = 1|x)$ is the probability of the positive class given the input features x.

Patterson's Vision for the Future of ML and AI

Looking ahead, Patterson envisions a future where ML and AI will continue to integrate seamlessly into everyday life, enhancing decision-making processes and automating tasks across various sectors. He believes that the convergence of AI with other emerging technologies, such as quantum computing, will unlock unprecedented capabilities.

In his view, the ethical considerations surrounding AI development are paramount. Patterson advocates for responsible AI practices that prioritize transparency, fairness, and accountability. He emphasizes the need for interdisciplinary collaboration to address the societal impacts of AI technologies, ensuring that they serve humanity positively.

In summary, David Patterson's venture into Machine Learning and AI underscores his commitment to innovation and his belief in the transformative power of technology. Through his contributions, he has laid the groundwork for future advancements in these fields, inspiring a new generation of technologists to explore the limitless possibilities of AI.

Patterson's Approach to Collaborative Research

David Patterson's approach to collaborative research is a testament to his belief that innovation thrives in an environment where diverse ideas and perspectives intersect. Throughout his illustrious career, Patterson has championed collaborative efforts that not only enhance the quality of research but also broaden its impact across various domains of technology.

Theoretical Foundations of Collaboration

At the core of Patterson's collaborative philosophy lies the understanding that complex problems in technology often require multidisciplinary solutions. This perspective aligns with the theory of *Collective Intelligence*, which posits that groups can outperform individuals in problem-solving tasks. As noted by Malone and Bernstein (2015), "the ability of groups to solve problems is often greater than that of individuals working alone." Patterson's work exemplifies this theory, particularly in the realms of computer architecture and artificial intelligence.

Collaborative Frameworks

Patterson employs several frameworks to facilitate collaboration, including:

- **Interdisciplinary Teams:** By assembling teams from various fields such as computer science, neuroscience, and robotics, Patterson fosters an environment where innovative ideas can flourish. For instance, his collaboration with neuroscientists has led to breakthroughs in neuromorphic computing, which mimics neural structures to improve processing efficiency.

- **Open Source Initiatives:** Patterson is a strong advocate for open-source software, believing that transparency and accessibility can accelerate technological advancements. The RISC-V project is a prime example, where Patterson invited researchers and companies to contribute to the development of an open standard for instruction set architectures.

- **Industry Partnerships:** Collaborating with industry leaders such as Intel and NVIDIA, Patterson has bridged the gap between academia and industry, ensuring that theoretical advancements can be translated into practical applications.

Addressing Challenges in Collaboration

While collaboration offers numerous benefits, it is not without challenges. Patterson has encountered issues such as differing priorities among stakeholders, intellectual property concerns, and the integration of diverse methodologies. To address these challenges, he emphasizes the importance of clear communication and shared goals.

By establishing common objectives at the outset of a project, Patterson ensures that all collaborators are aligned in their vision.

Case Studies of Collaborative Success

One notable instance of Patterson's collaborative research is the development of the RISC architecture itself. In partnership with John L. Hennessy, Patterson conducted extensive research that culminated in the publication of their seminal work, "Computer Architecture: A Quantitative Approach." This collaboration not only advanced the field of computer architecture but also set a new standard for academic publishing, demonstrating how teamwork can lead to groundbreaking discoveries.

Another significant example is Patterson's involvement in the RISC-V Foundation, which promotes the RISC-V instruction set architecture. By rallying a global community of researchers and engineers, Patterson has fostered an ecosystem that encourages contributions from diverse sectors, including academia, industry, and hobbyists. This collaborative approach has resulted in rapid advancements in open-source hardware and has inspired a new generation of engineers.

Conclusion

David Patterson's approach to collaborative research exemplifies the power of collective intelligence in driving technological innovation. By fostering interdisciplinary teams, advocating for open-source initiatives, and forming strategic industry partnerships, Patterson has not only advanced the field of computer architecture but has also set a precedent for future research collaborations. As technology continues to evolve, Patterson's commitment to collaboration will undoubtedly inspire new breakthroughs and shape the future of the industry.

Bibliography

[1] Malone, T. W., & Bernstein, M. S. (2015). *Handbook of Collective Intelligence*. MIT Press.

The Intersection of Computer Science and Neuroscience

The intersection of computer science and neuroscience is a dynamic and rapidly evolving field that explores how computational models can be used to understand the brain's complex functions and, conversely, how insights from neuroscience can inform the development of artificial intelligence (AI) and machine learning (ML). This synergy between two seemingly disparate disciplines has given rise to innovative approaches in both understanding human cognition and advancing technology.

Neuroscience Fundamentals

Neuroscience is the scientific study of the nervous system, encompassing various subfields such as neuroanatomy, neurophysiology, neurobiology, and cognitive neuroscience. The core unit of the nervous system is the neuron, which communicates through electrical impulses and neurotransmitter release. Neurons form networks that process information through synaptic connections, leading to complex behaviors and cognitive functions.

$$V(t) = V_{rest} + \frac{g_{Na}}{C_m}(E_{Na} - V(t)) - \frac{g_K}{C_m}(V(t) - E_K) \tag{78}$$

In this equation, $V(t)$ represents the membrane potential of a neuron at time t, V_{rest} is the resting potential, g_{Na} and g_K are the conductances for sodium and potassium ions, respectively, E_{Na} and E_K are the equilibrium potentials for sodium and potassium ions, and C_m is the membrane capacitance. This mathematical representation of neuronal behavior is fundamental to understanding how electrical signals propagate through neural networks.

Computational Models of the Brain

Computational neuroscience employs mathematical models and simulations to replicate neural processes. One prominent model is the Hodgkin-Huxley model, which describes how action potentials in neurons are initiated and propagated. This model has been instrumental in elucidating the dynamics of neuronal firing and synaptic transmission.

Another approach is the use of artificial neural networks (ANNs), which are inspired by biological neural networks. ANNs consist of interconnected nodes (neurons) that process inputs and produce outputs, mimicking the way biological systems learn from experience. The architecture of ANNs can vary significantly, from simple feedforward networks to complex recurrent networks that can model temporal dependencies.

$$y = f\left(\sum_{i=1}^{n} w_i x_i + b\right) \tag{79}$$

In this equation, y is the output of the neuron, f is an activation function (such as sigmoid or ReLU), w_i are the weights associated with each input x_i, and b is the bias term. The learning process in ANNs involves adjusting these weights and biases through algorithms like backpropagation.

Neuroinformatics and Big Data

The field of neuroinformatics combines neuroscience data with computational tools to analyze and model brain activity. With the advent of advanced imaging techniques, such as functional magnetic resonance imaging (fMRI) and electroencephalography (EEG), vast amounts of data are generated, necessitating sophisticated computational methods for analysis.

Neuroinformatics platforms, such as the Allen Brain Atlas, provide repositories for brain data that can be utilized for research and modeling. These platforms enable researchers to visualize brain structures, understand functional connectivity, and explore the genetic basis of neural function.

Applications in Artificial Intelligence

The insights gained from neuroscience have significantly influenced the development of AI. For instance, concepts such as reinforcement learning draw parallels to how humans and animals learn from their environment through trial and error. In reinforcement learning, an agent learns to make decisions by receiving rewards or penalties based on its actions, similar to the way dopamine signals reward in the brain.

Moreover, the development of convolutional neural networks (CNNs) has been inspired by the visual processing pathways in the brain. CNNs are designed to recognize patterns in visual data, effectively mimicking the hierarchical processing observed in the visual cortex.

$$\text{Output} = \sigma\left(W * X + b\right) \tag{80}$$

In this equation, W represents the filter weights, X is the input image, b is the bias, and σ is the activation function. The convolution operation $*$ allows the network to extract features from the input, akin to how the brain processes visual information.

Ethical Considerations and Future Directions

As the intersection of computer science and neuroscience continues to expand, ethical considerations become increasingly important. Issues surrounding data privacy, the implications of AI in decision-making, and the potential for neurotechnology to influence human behavior raise critical questions about the responsible use of these technologies.

Future directions in this field include the development of brain-computer interfaces (BCIs), which aim to create direct communication pathways between the brain and external devices. This technology holds promise for applications in rehabilitation, assistive devices, and even enhancing cognitive functions.

In conclusion, the intersection of computer science and neuroscience is a rich and fertile ground for innovation, blending the understanding of biological systems with advanced computational techniques. As researchers continue to explore this synergy, the potential for groundbreaking discoveries and transformative technologies remains vast.

Contributions to Robotics and Automation

David Patterson's journey into the realm of robotics and automation is a testament to his innovative spirit and commitment to pushing the boundaries of technology. As a pioneer in computer architecture, Patterson recognized early on the transformative potential of integrating advanced computing techniques into robotic systems. This section delves into Patterson's contributions to this field, examining the theoretical foundations, practical applications, and the challenges he faced along the way.

Theoretical Foundations

At the core of Patterson's contributions to robotics lies the application of the Reduced Instruction Set Computer (RISC) architecture. RISC principles emphasize a small set of instructions that execute rapidly, allowing for efficient processing in real-time applications. This efficiency is crucial for robotics, where timely decision-making can mean the difference between success and failure.

The RISC architecture can be mathematically represented as:

$$\text{Execution Time} = \frac{\text{Number of Instructions}}{\text{Clock Rate}} \times \text{Cycles per Instruction} \tag{81}$$

In robotics, where tasks often require complex computations, the ability to minimize execution time through optimized instruction sets becomes essential. Patterson's work on RISC not only provided a blueprint for designing faster processors but also laid the groundwork for the development of specialized processors tailored for robotic applications.

Practical Applications

Patterson's influence is evident in various robotic systems developed during his career. One notable example is the use of RISC processors in autonomous vehicles. These vehicles rely on sophisticated algorithms for navigation, obstacle detection, and decision-making. By leveraging the efficiency of RISC architecture, engineers can create systems that process vast amounts of sensor data in real time.

For instance, in a self-driving car, the ability to quickly analyze data from LIDAR, cameras, and radar is paramount. The integration of RISC processors allows for the rapid execution of algorithms such as simultaneous localization and mapping (SLAM), which is crucial for the vehicle's ability to understand its environment.

Challenges in Robotics

Despite the advantages of RISC architecture in robotics, Patterson faced significant challenges in the adoption of these technologies. One major hurdle was the resistance from traditionalists who favored complex instruction set computing (CISC) architectures. Critics argued that CISC could handle more complex tasks with fewer instructions, making it more suitable for certain robotic applications.

To address these concerns, Patterson and his collaborators conducted extensive research demonstrating the advantages of RISC in specific robotic contexts. They showed that while CISC might excel in certain scenarios, RISC's streamlined approach often resulted in superior performance in real-time applications. This research culminated in several influential papers and presentations that helped shift the perception of RISC in the robotics community.

Collaborative Innovations

Patterson's contributions to robotics were not limited to theoretical advancements; he also actively engaged in collaborative projects that pushed the envelope of what robots could achieve. One such project involved partnering with researchers in the fields of artificial intelligence and machine learning to develop intelligent robotic systems capable of learning from their environments.

These projects often incorporated techniques such as reinforcement learning, where robots learn to make decisions based on feedback from their actions. Patterson's insights into efficient processing allowed for the implementation of these algorithms in real-time, enabling robots to adapt and improve their performance over time.

For example, in a collaborative project aimed at developing robotic arms for manufacturing, Patterson's team utilized RISC processors to enhance the speed and accuracy of the robotic movements. The result was a system that could adjust its actions based on the variability of the materials it was handling, leading to increased efficiency in production lines.

Future Directions in Robotics

Looking ahead, Patterson's vision for the future of robotics and automation is intertwined with the advancement of RISC architecture and its derivatives. The emergence of RISC-V, an open standard instruction set architecture, presents new opportunities for innovation in robotic systems. By promoting an open-source approach, Patterson aims to democratize access to advanced robotics technologies, fostering collaboration and creativity across diverse fields.

The potential applications of RISC-V in robotics are vast. From drones that can navigate complex environments autonomously to collaborative robots (cobots) working alongside humans in factories, the future is bright. Patterson's emphasis on efficiency, adaptability, and accessibility will continue to shape the trajectory of robotics and automation.

Conclusion

David Patterson's contributions to robotics and automation exemplify the profound impact of computer architecture on practical applications. By championing the principles of RISC, he has not only advanced the field of robotics but has also inspired a new generation of engineers and researchers to explore the limitless possibilities of technology. As we move forward, Patterson's legacy will undoubtedly influence the next wave of innovations in robotics, paving the way for smarter, more efficient systems that enhance our lives in countless ways.

Implications for the Future of Work

As we delve into the implications of David Patterson's work on the future of work, it is essential to recognize the transformative impact of computer architecture, particularly through the lens of RISC (Reduced Instruction Set Computer) architecture. Patterson's innovations have not only redefined how computers operate but have also set the stage for a new era of automation, efficiency, and collaboration in the workplace.

The Shift Towards Automation

One of the most significant implications of Patterson's contributions is the acceleration of automation across various industries. With the advent of RISC architecture, processors have become more efficient, enabling faster data processing and execution of complex algorithms. This efficiency has paved the way for advanced automation technologies, such as robotics and artificial intelligence (AI), which are increasingly integrated into everyday work environments.

For instance, consider the manufacturing sector, where automation has revolutionized production lines. According to a report by McKinsey Global Institute, automation could raise productivity globally by 0.8 to 1.4 percent annually. The efficiency gains from RISC-based systems empower machines to perform tasks previously reserved for human workers, leading to increased output and reduced operational costs.

The Rise of Remote Work

Patterson's influence extends beyond automation; it also encompasses the evolution of remote work. The efficiency and power of RISC processors have facilitated the development of cloud computing and collaborative software tools, enabling seamless communication and collaboration regardless of geographical boundaries. As a result, remote work has become a viable option for many professionals, reshaping traditional office dynamics.

The COVID-19 pandemic accelerated this shift, with many companies adopting remote work policies. A survey by Gartner found that 74% of CFOs intend to shift some employees to remote work permanently. This transition has led to a reevaluation of workplace culture, productivity metrics, and employee engagement strategies.

New Skill Requirements

As automation and remote work become more prevalent, the demand for new skill sets will emerge. Workers will need to adapt to technological advancements and develop competencies that complement automated systems. This shift necessitates a focus on continuous learning and upskilling, as traditional job roles evolve or become obsolete.

For example, jobs that require creativity, emotional intelligence, and complex problem-solving are becoming more valuable, as these skills cannot be easily replicated by machines. Patterson's advocacy for open-source technology encourages educational institutions and organizations to foster a culture of innovation and collaboration, equipping workers with the skills needed to thrive in an automated future.

Ethical Considerations and Job Displacement

While the advancements in technology present numerous benefits, they also raise ethical concerns, particularly regarding job displacement. As RISC architecture enhances automation, there is a legitimate fear that many jobs may be rendered obsolete. A study by the World Economic Forum predicts that by 2025, 85 million jobs may be displaced by automation, while 97 million new roles could emerge.

Patterson's commitment to accessible technology and ethical considerations in his work emphasizes the need for a balanced approach to automation. It is crucial for policymakers, educators, and industry leaders to collaborate in creating strategies that mitigate the negative impacts of job displacement. This includes investing in retraining programs and developing social safety nets for affected workers.

The Future of Collaboration and Innovation

Finally, Patterson's vision for the future of technology highlights the importance of collaboration and innovation in the workplace. The integration of RISC architecture into various fields fosters an environment where interdisciplinary teams can thrive. By leveraging the capabilities of advanced computing, professionals from diverse backgrounds can collaborate on projects that push the boundaries of innovation.

For example, the intersection of computer science and neuroscience, as explored by Patterson, has the potential to revolutionize fields such as healthcare and education. Collaborative research initiatives that combine expertise from different disciplines can lead to groundbreaking discoveries and solutions to complex societal challenges.

Conclusion

In conclusion, the implications of David Patterson's work on the future of work are profound and multifaceted. From the rise of automation and remote work to the need for new skills and ethical considerations, Patterson's contributions to computer architecture have set the stage for a rapidly evolving workforce. As we navigate these changes, it is essential to embrace a collaborative and innovative mindset, ensuring that technology serves as a tool for empowerment and progress in the workplace.

$$\text{Future Productivity} = \text{Automation Efficiency} \times \text{Workforce Adaptability} \quad (82)$$

Patterson's Quest for Sustainable Technologies

In an era where environmental concerns dominate global discourse, David Patterson's commitment to sustainable technologies has emerged as a defining aspect of his illustrious career. As the architect of the Reduced Instruction Set Computer (RISC) architecture, Patterson has long recognized the potential of computing to drive efficiency not only in processing power but also in energy consumption. This section explores Patterson's innovative approaches to sustainable technology, the challenges he faced, and the implications of his work for the future of the tech industry.

The Importance of Sustainability in Technology

The intersection of technology and sustainability is critical in addressing pressing global issues such as climate change, resource depletion, and energy inefficiency. Patterson's philosophy is rooted in the belief that technological advancements should not only enhance performance but also minimize environmental impact. This perspective is crucial, as the tech industry is responsible for a significant portion of global energy consumption. According to a report by the International

Energy Agency (IEA), data centers alone consumed about 200 terawatt-hours (TWh) of electricity in 2018, accounting for roughly 1% of global energy demand [?].

Innovative Approaches to Sustainable Computing

Patterson's quest for sustainable technologies is exemplified through several key initiatives and research projects aimed at reducing energy consumption in computing. One of the most notable contributions is the development of energy-efficient processor architectures. The RISC philosophy emphasizes simplicity and efficiency, allowing for higher performance per watt. This efficiency is quantified using the following equation:

$$\text{Performance per Watt} = \frac{\text{Performance (MIPS)}}{\text{Power Consumption (Watts)}} \tag{83}$$

By optimizing the RISC architecture, Patterson and his collaborators demonstrated that it is possible to achieve significant performance gains while simultaneously reducing power requirements.

Challenges in Sustainable Technology Development

Despite Patterson's innovative vision, the journey toward sustainable technology is fraught with challenges. One significant hurdle is the industry's reliance on proprietary systems that prioritize performance over energy efficiency. Many companies are hesitant to adopt open-source architectures like RISC-V due to concerns about competitive advantage and intellectual property. Patterson has been a vocal advocate for open-source solutions, arguing that they can foster collaboration and accelerate the development of sustainable technologies.

Moreover, the rapid pace of technological advancement often leads to a cycle of obsolescence, where devices are discarded long before their useful life has ended. This contributes to electronic waste (e-waste), which poses severe environmental risks. Patterson's response to this challenge has been to promote designs that prioritize longevity and recyclability, encouraging manufacturers to consider the entire lifecycle of their products.

Real-World Applications and Impact

One of the most impactful examples of Patterson's commitment to sustainable technologies is his involvement with the RISC-V Foundation. RISC-V is an open standard instruction set architecture that promotes energy-efficient computing. By providing a platform for collaboration, RISC-V allows researchers and companies to develop processors tailored for specific applications, including low-power devices for the Internet of Things (IoT). These devices are essential for creating smart, connected environments that can optimize energy usage across various sectors.

For instance, IoT devices powered by RISC-V architecture can be deployed in smart homes to monitor and manage energy consumption in real-time. By leveraging machine learning algorithms, these devices can predict usage patterns and adjust settings accordingly, leading to substantial energy savings. Patterson's vision for RISC-V extends beyond traditional computing, aiming to revolutionize sectors such as healthcare, agriculture, and transportation through sustainable technology.

The Future of Sustainable Technologies

As we look to the future, Patterson's quest for sustainable technologies continues to inspire a new generation of technologists and researchers. His advocacy for open-source solutions and energy-efficient architectures serves as a blueprint for addressing the environmental challenges posed by the tech industry. The ongoing development of RISC-V and its adoption across various sectors underscores the potential for sustainable computing to reshape our world.

In conclusion, David Patterson's commitment to sustainable technologies reflects a profound understanding of the role that computing plays in our society. By prioritizing energy efficiency and advocating for open-source solutions, Patterson is not only shaping the future of computer architecture but also ensuring that technology serves as a force for good in addressing global challenges. His legacy will undoubtedly inspire future innovators to pursue sustainable practices in their work, fostering a more environmentally responsible tech industry.

Exploring the Frontiers of Quantum Computing

Quantum computing represents a paradigm shift in computation, leveraging the principles of quantum mechanics to process information in ways that classical computers cannot. At the heart of quantum computing lies the quantum bit, or qubit, which differs fundamentally from the classical bit. A classical bit can exist in one of two states, 0 or 1, whereas a qubit can exist in a superposition of both states simultaneously, described mathematically as:

$$|\psi\rangle = \alpha|0\rangle + \beta|1\rangle \tag{84}$$

where α and β are complex numbers that satisfy the normalization condition $|\alpha|^2 + |\beta|^2 = 1$. This property allows quantum computers to perform multiple calculations at once, exponentially increasing their processing power for certain tasks.

Quantum Entanglement

A key feature of quantum computing is entanglement, a phenomenon where qubits become interconnected such that the state of one qubit cannot be described independently of the state of another, no matter the distance between them. Mathematically, if two qubits are entangled, their joint state can be expressed as:

$$|\Psi\rangle = \frac{1}{\sqrt{2}}(|00\rangle + |11\rangle) \tag{85}$$

This entangled state leads to correlations between measurements of the qubits, which can be exploited in quantum algorithms, such as Shor's algorithm for factoring large integers and Grover's algorithm for searching unsorted databases.

Quantum Algorithms

The development of quantum algorithms has been one of the most exciting aspects of quantum computing. Shor's algorithm, for instance, demonstrates how quantum computers can factor large numbers efficiently, posing a potential threat to classical encryption methods. The algorithm operates in polynomial time, as opposed to the exponential time required by the best-known classical algorithms. The core of Shor's algorithm involves the quantum Fourier transform, which can be expressed as:

$$QFT(|x\rangle) = \frac{1}{\sqrt{N}} \sum_{k=0}^{N-1} e^{2\pi ixk/N} |k\rangle \tag{86}$$

where N is the size of the input. This transformation allows the extraction of periodicity from quantum states, which is crucial for factoring.

Grover's algorithm, on the other hand, provides a quadratic speedup for unstructured search problems. It can find a specific item in an unsorted database of N items in $O(\sqrt{N})$ time, compared to the classical $O(N)$. The algorithm iteratively applies a series of operations known as the Grover iteration, defined as:

$$G = (2|\psi\rangle\langle\psi| - I) \cdot U_f \tag{87}$$

where U_f is the oracle that marks the correct solution, and I is the identity operator. The power of Grover's algorithm lies in its ability to amplify the probability of measuring the correct solution.

Challenges in Quantum Computing

Despite the theoretical advantages of quantum computing, several challenges remain. One major issue is decoherence, where the fragile quantum states lose their coherence due to interaction with the environment. This can lead to errors in computation. Quantum error correction codes, such as the surface code, are being developed to mitigate these errors. The surface code can be represented as:

$$H = \sum_p (1 - Z_p) \tag{88}$$

where Z_p is the stabilizer operator for a given plaquette p. These codes allow for fault-tolerant quantum computation, enabling the reliable execution of quantum algorithms.

Another challenge is the scalability of quantum systems. Current quantum computers, such as those developed by IBM and Google, have a limited number of qubits. The quest for a scalable quantum architecture involves exploring various physical implementations, including superconducting qubits, trapped ions, and topological qubits.

Real-World Applications of Quantum Computing

The potential applications of quantum computing are vast and span various fields. In cryptography, quantum computing could break widely-used encryption schemes, prompting the development of quantum-resistant algorithms. In materials science, quantum simulations can lead to the discovery of new materials with desirable properties, such as superconductivity at higher temperatures.

In the field of medicine, quantum computing can accelerate drug discovery by simulating molecular interactions at an unprecedented level of detail. For instance, quantum algorithms can model complex biochemical systems, leading to insights that classical computers cannot achieve.

The Future of Quantum Computing

As researchers continue to explore the frontiers of quantum computing, the vision for the future is one of hybrid systems where quantum and classical computing coexist. Quantum computers will handle specific tasks that benefit from their unique capabilities, while classical systems will continue to manage everyday computing needs.

Patterson's contributions to this field are significant, as he encourages collaboration between academia and industry to drive innovation in quantum technologies. His vision includes fostering a new generation of researchers who will push the boundaries of what is possible in computing.

In conclusion, quantum computing stands at the precipice of revolutionizing technology as we know it. With its theoretical underpinnings, groundbreaking algorithms, and real-world applications, the exploration of quantum computing will undoubtedly shape the future of not only computer science but also various domains of human endeavor.

Challenges Faced in Pursuit of New Innovations

In the ever-evolving landscape of technology, David Patterson's journey in pursuit of new innovations has been fraught with challenges that tested his resolve and creativity. This section delves into the myriad obstacles Patterson faced, from technical limitations to industry resistance, and how he navigated these hurdles to push the boundaries of computer architecture and technology.

1. Technical Limitations

One of the primary challenges Patterson encountered was the inherent technical limitations of existing hardware and software systems. As he sought to develop the RISC (Reduced Instruction Set Computing) architecture, he often faced constraints related to processing power, memory bandwidth, and energy efficiency. These limitations necessitated innovative approaches to design and implementation.

For instance, in the early stages of RISC development, Patterson and his team recognized that traditional CISC (Complex Instruction Set Computing) architectures were becoming increasingly inefficient. The RISC philosophy promoted a simpler set of instructions, allowing for faster execution times. However, this shift required overcoming the initial skepticism from the industry, which was heavily invested in CISC architectures.

The equation that encapsulates the trade-offs between performance and complexity in processor design can be represented as:

$$\text{Performance} \propto \frac{\text{Instructions Executed}}{\text{Cycles per Instruction} \times \text{Cycle Time}}$$

This equation highlights the need for a balance between the number of instructions and their execution efficiency, a challenge that Patterson had to address head-on.

2. Industry Resistance

Patterson's advocacy for RISC architecture was met with considerable resistance from established industry players. The dominance of proprietary systems created a landscape where innovation was often stifled by the status quo. Companies that had invested heavily in CISC architectures were reluctant to embrace the RISC model, fearing that it would undermine their existing products and market share.

The backlash from industry leaders manifested in various forms, including public criticism and attempts to discredit RISC's viability. Patterson's response was to engage in rigorous research and empirical validation of RISC's advantages. He conducted extensive benchmarking studies that demonstrated the performance benefits of RISC over CISC, effectively countering the skepticism surrounding his work.

3. Funding and Resource Allocation

Securing funding and resources for innovative projects has always been a significant challenge in the tech industry. Patterson faced difficulties in obtaining financial backing for his research initiatives, particularly when proposing projects that deviated from established norms. The need for funding was critical, as pioneering research often requires substantial investment in technology, personnel, and infrastructure.

To address this challenge, Patterson leveraged his academic connections and sought partnerships with industry stakeholders who recognized the potential of RISC architecture. Collaborations with universities and tech companies not only provided the necessary funding but also facilitated knowledge exchange and resource sharing.

4. Balancing Innovation with Practicality

Another challenge Patterson faced was the delicate balance between innovation and practicality. While pushing the boundaries of technology, it was essential to ensure that new innovations were feasible and could be implemented effectively in real-world applications. This required a deep understanding of market needs and technological trends.

Patterson's approach involved iterative design and prototyping, allowing him to refine his ideas based on feedback from peers and industry experts. For instance, the development of RISC processors involved multiple iterations, where each version incorporated lessons learned from previous models. This iterative process is crucial in mitigating risks associated with new technology adoption.

5. Ethical Considerations

As technology advanced, Patterson encountered ethical dilemmas related to the implications of his innovations. The rise of artificial intelligence (AI) and machine learning (ML) brought forth concerns regarding privacy, security, and the potential for misuse of technology. Patterson recognized the importance of addressing these ethical considerations in his work.

In his collaborations, he emphasized the need for responsible innovation, advocating for transparency and accountability in technological advancements. Patterson's commitment to ethical practices was evident in his involvement with organizations focused on promoting diversity and inclusivity in tech, ensuring that innovations benefitted society as a whole.

6. Competition and Market Dynamics

The competitive nature of the tech industry posed another significant challenge for Patterson. As he championed RISC architecture, numerous competitors emerged, each vying for a share of the market. This intense competition often led to rapid technological advancements, making it imperative for Patterson to stay ahead of the curve.

To maintain a competitive edge, Patterson continuously explored emerging technologies and trends, such as quantum computing and neuromorphic engineering. By anticipating market shifts, he positioned himself and his work at the forefront of innovation, ensuring that RISC remained relevant in an ever-changing landscape.

7. Personal Sacrifices

Pursuing groundbreaking innovations often requires personal sacrifices. Patterson's commitment to his work sometimes meant long hours, travel for conferences, and a demanding schedule that left little time for personal life. The pressure to deliver results weighed heavily on him, leading to moments of self-doubt and stress.

Despite these challenges, Patterson found solace in his passion for technology and the impact it could have on the world. His resilience and determination to overcome personal obstacles fueled his drive to innovate, reminding him of the importance of balance and self-care in sustaining a successful career.

8. Conclusion

In summary, the pursuit of new innovations is fraught with challenges that require a multifaceted approach to overcome. David Patterson's journey exemplifies the resilience and creativity needed to navigate technical limitations, industry resistance, funding constraints, ethical considerations, and personal sacrifices. By embracing these challenges, Patterson not only advanced the field of computer architecture but also inspired future generations to push the boundaries of what is possible in technology.

Through his work, Patterson demonstrated that innovation is not merely about creating new technologies; it is about addressing the challenges that arise in the pursuit of progress. His legacy serves as a testament to the power of perseverance and the importance of ethical considerations in shaping the future of technology.

Patterson's Vision for the Future of Technology

David Patterson, a luminary in the realm of computer architecture, has consistently pushed the boundaries of what technology can achieve. His vision for the future is not merely about advancing hardware capabilities but also about fostering an ecosystem where technology serves humanity in meaningful and sustainable ways. This section delves into Patterson's forward-looking perspectives, highlighting the theoretical frameworks, potential problems, and illustrative examples that shape his vision.

Theoretical Frameworks

At the core of Patterson's vision lies the principle of **open architecture**, which emphasizes the importance of accessibility and collaboration in technological advancement. This concept is rooted in the belief that innovation thrives in an environment where ideas can be freely exchanged and built upon. Patterson's advocacy for open-source technologies, particularly through the RISC-V initiative, exemplifies this ethos. The RISC-V architecture, being open and extensible, allows researchers and developers worldwide to contribute to its evolution, fostering a collaborative spirit that can lead to groundbreaking innovations.

$$\text{Innovation} = f(\text{Collaboration}, \text{Accessibility}, \text{Diversity}) \tag{89}$$

This equation encapsulates Patterson's belief that innovation is a function of collaboration among diverse groups, enabled by accessible platforms and resources. By democratizing access to technology, Patterson envisions a future where individuals from all walks of life can contribute to and benefit from technological advancements.

Addressing Global Challenges

Patterson's vision is also heavily influenced by the pressing global challenges of our time, such as climate change, inequality, and access to education. He believes that technology should play a pivotal role in addressing these issues. For instance, Patterson has actively promoted the development of **sustainable technologies** that minimize environmental impact. His work in energy-efficient computing is a testament to this commitment. By designing processors that consume less power without sacrificing performance, Patterson aims to reduce the carbon footprint of computing technologies.

$$\text{Energy Efficiency} = \frac{\text{Performance}}{\text{Power Consumption}} \tag{90}$$

This equation highlights the importance of energy efficiency in computing. Patterson's vision includes a future where processors are not only powerful but also environmentally responsible, contributing to a sustainable technological landscape.

The Role of Artificial Intelligence

Another cornerstone of Patterson's vision is the integration of **artificial intelligence** (AI) into everyday applications. He recognizes that AI has the potential to revolutionize industries, improve quality of life, and enhance decision-making processes. Patterson advocates for the development of AI systems that are not only powerful but also ethical and transparent. He emphasizes the need for AI to be designed with a focus on human values, ensuring that technology serves to empower individuals rather than diminish their autonomy.

$$\text{AI Ethics} = f(\text{Transparency}, \text{Fairness}, \text{Accountability}) \tag{91}$$

This equation underscores Patterson's belief that ethical AI must be built on principles of transparency, fairness, and accountability. By prioritizing these values, Patterson envisions a future where AI technologies are trusted and beneficial to society.

Education and Workforce Development

Patterson also places significant emphasis on **education** and workforce development as crucial components of his vision for the future. He believes that to harness the full potential of technology, we must invest in education systems that prepare individuals for the demands of a rapidly evolving job market. This includes promoting skills in computer science, data analysis, and critical thinking from an early age.

Patterson advocates for partnerships between academia and industry to create curricula that reflect real-world challenges and opportunities. By aligning educational outcomes with the needs of the workforce, he envisions a future where individuals are equipped with the skills necessary to thrive in a technology-driven economy.

Conclusion: A Holistic Approach

In conclusion, David Patterson's vision for the future of technology is characterized by a holistic approach that integrates open architecture, sustainability, ethical AI, and education. He envisions a world where technology is not just a tool for advancement but a means to foster collaboration, address global challenges, and empower individuals. As we look ahead, Patterson's insights serve as a guiding light for the next generation of technologists, urging them to innovate responsibly and inclusively.

Through this vision, Patterson inspires us to imagine a future where technology and humanity coexist harmoniously, driving progress while respecting the planet and its inhabitants. The journey towards this future is fraught with challenges, but with leaders like Patterson at the helm, there is hope that we can navigate these complexities and emerge stronger and more united.

Chapter Three: The Human Side of a Tech Guru

Section One: Life Outside the Computer Lab

Patterson's Interests and Hobbies

David Patterson, the architect of RISC, is not just a genius in the realm of computer architecture; he is also a multifaceted individual with a wide array of interests and hobbies that reflect his vibrant personality. While his contributions to computing are monumental, it is his passion for life outside of the lab that adds depth to his character and inspires those around him.

A Love for Music

One of Patterson's most cherished hobbies is music. Growing up in a household where creativity was celebrated, he found solace in melodies and rhythms. Whether it was strumming a guitar or attending live performances, music has always been a significant part of his life. His eclectic taste ranges from classical composers like Bach to contemporary artists, mirroring his appreciation for both tradition and innovation.

This passion for music not only serves as a creative outlet but also provides him with a mental break from the rigorous demands of his work. As Patterson once stated, "Music is like coding; it requires a blend of structure and improvisation." This analogy highlights his belief in the parallels between these two seemingly different worlds.

Outdoor Adventures

Another notable interest of Patterson's is his love for the outdoors. An avid hiker and nature enthusiast, he often seeks refuge in the great outdoors, finding inspiration in the beauty of nature. The tranquility of hiking trails and the thrill of mountain climbing allow him to disconnect from the fast-paced tech environment and recharge his creative batteries.

Patterson's adventures in the wilderness are not just about physical activity; they also serve as a source of reflection and inspiration. He often draws parallels between the challenges faced in nature and those encountered in technology. For instance, navigating a difficult trail can be likened to debugging a complex piece of code—both require patience, perseverance, and a clear vision of the end goal.

Culinary Arts

In addition to music and outdoor activities, Patterson has a keen interest in culinary arts. He enjoys experimenting with different cuisines and flavors, often hosting dinner parties for friends and colleagues. Cooking, for him, is an art form that requires precision, creativity, and a dash of spontaneity—much like programming.

His culinary adventures often lead to delightful discoveries, such as perfecting a homemade pasta recipe or mastering the art of baking bread. Patterson believes that cooking is a way to connect with others and share experiences, much like how collaboration in technology fosters innovation and progress.

Reading and Continuous Learning

Patterson is also a voracious reader, with a particular fondness for science fiction and biographies of influential figures in technology and science. He believes that reading not only broadens one's perspective but also fuels creativity and innovation. Titles such as "The Innovators" by Walter Isaacson and "Gödel, Escher, Bach" by Douglas Hofstadter have profoundly influenced his thinking.

He often emphasizes the importance of continuous learning, stating, "The moment you stop learning is the moment you stop growing." This philosophy drives him to explore new topics, whether through formal education or self-study, ensuring that he remains at the forefront of technological advancements.

Community Engagement and Mentorship

Beyond personal interests, Patterson is deeply committed to community engagement and mentorship. He actively participates in initiatives aimed at encouraging young people to pursue careers in STEM (Science, Technology, Engineering, and Mathematics). Through workshops, speaking engagements, and hands-on projects, he strives to inspire the next generation of innovators.

Patterson believes that sharing knowledge is one of the most rewarding aspects of his career. He often recalls moments when a student's "aha" moment ignited a spark of curiosity, reinforcing his commitment to fostering a love for technology in others.

Conclusion

In summary, David Patterson's interests and hobbies paint a picture of a well-rounded individual who embraces life with enthusiasm and creativity. His love for music, outdoor adventures, culinary arts, reading, and community engagement not only enrich his personal life but also enhance his professional endeavors. These passions reflect his belief that a balanced life fosters innovation and creativity, ultimately leading to greater contributions to the field of technology and beyond.

Balancing Work and Personal Life

In the fast-paced world of technology, where innovation is the driving force, the balance between work and personal life can often become a tightrope walk. For David Patterson, a luminary in computer architecture, this balancing act was not just a personal challenge but a professional necessity. The pursuit of excellence in the tech field often comes at the expense of personal time and relationships. This section explores Patterson's strategies for maintaining equilibrium in his life while navigating the demands of his career.

Theoretical Framework

The concept of work-life balance is grounded in various psychological and sociological theories. One prominent theory is the **Boundary Theory**, which posits that individuals create boundaries between their work and personal lives to manage their time and responsibilities effectively [?]. These boundaries can be physical, temporal, or psychological, and their management is crucial for mental well-being.

Another relevant framework is the **Work-Family Conflict Theory**, which suggests that the demands of work and family can be mutually incompatible, leading to stress and dissatisfaction [?]. Patterson's experience exemplifies the struggle between professional obligations and personal commitments, making it essential to explore how he navigated these challenges.

Challenges Faced

Despite his significant contributions to the field, Patterson faced numerous challenges in balancing his work and personal life. The demands of academia, including research deadlines, teaching responsibilities, and collaboration with industry leaders, often consumed his time. The pressure to publish groundbreaking research and maintain a reputation as a thought leader in computer architecture added to this burden.

For example, during the early years of developing the RISC architecture, Patterson often found himself working late into the night, sacrificing family dinners and social outings. The intense focus required for such pioneering work sometimes led to feelings of isolation and burnout, a common experience among high-achieving professionals in the tech industry [?].

Strategies for Balance

To counteract the pressures of his career, Patterson adopted several strategies aimed at achieving a healthier work-life balance. One of the key approaches was establishing **clear boundaries** between work and personal time. He set specific hours for work and committed to unplugging from technology during family time. This practice not only allowed him to be present with his loved ones but also provided him with the mental space needed to recharge.

Additionally, Patterson emphasized the importance of **delegation and collaboration**. By fostering a collaborative environment in his research teams, he could share responsibilities and reduce the burden on himself. This teamwork not only enhanced productivity but also allowed him to mentor younger researchers, creating a supportive community within the tech landscape.

Examples of Balance

Patterson's dedication to balance is evident in his personal life. He made time for hobbies such as hiking and photography, which provided a creative outlet and a break from the rigors of academia. These activities not only enriched his personal life but also contributed to his professional creativity, allowing him to approach problems with a fresh perspective.

Moreover, Patterson's commitment to education and mentorship extended beyond his professional obligations. He actively participated in community outreach programs aimed at inspiring the next generation of technologists. This involvement not only fulfilled his desire to give back but also enriched his own life by connecting him with passionate young minds.

Conclusion

In conclusion, balancing work and personal life is a complex challenge faced by many in the tech industry, and David Patterson's journey exemplifies this struggle. By implementing strategies such as setting boundaries, fostering collaboration, and engaging in personal interests, Patterson navigated the demands of his career while maintaining meaningful relationships and personal fulfillment. His story serves as an inspiration for others in the tech field, highlighting the importance of achieving a sustainable work-life balance in the pursuit of innovation and excellence.

Patterson's Circle of Friends and Mentors

David Patterson's journey through the tech landscape has been significantly shaped by a constellation of friends and mentors who have influenced his thinking, research, and professional growth. This section explores the pivotal relationships that have helped mold Patterson into the visionary he is today.

The Influence of Mentorship

Mentorship plays a crucial role in the development of any individual, especially in fields as dynamic and rapidly evolving as technology and computer science. For Patterson, mentors provided guidance, encouragement, and insight that helped him navigate the complexities of academia and industry. One of the most notable figures in Patterson's life was **John L. Hennessy**, who not only collaborated with Patterson on groundbreaking research but also served as a mentor during his formative years at the University of California, Berkeley. Hennessy's own work in computer architecture complemented Patterson's interests, allowing them to explore the innovative RISC (Reduced Instruction Set Computer) architecture together.

The mentor-mentee relationship can be quantified using the mentorship theory, which posits that effective mentorship enhances professional development through support, feedback, and modeling of behaviors. This model can be expressed as:

$$M = f(S, F, R) \tag{92}$$

where M represents the effectiveness of mentorship, S is the support provided, F denotes feedback, and R stands for the role modeling exhibited by the mentor. In Patterson's case, the combination of Hennessy's support, constructive feedback, and exemplary professional conduct significantly contributed to Patterson's early success.

Peer Relationships and Collaborative Spirit

In addition to formal mentorship, Patterson's circle includes a diverse group of peers who have been instrumental in his career. The collaborative environment fostered at Berkeley allowed Patterson to connect with other brilliant minds, including researchers like **David A. Patterson** (no relation) and **Mark Horowitz**. These relationships were characterized by a spirit of collaboration that is critical in the tech industry, where innovation often arises from collective efforts.

The collaborative approach is supported by the theory of social constructivism, which emphasizes that knowledge is constructed through social interactions. This can be represented as:

$$K = C + I \tag{93}$$

where K is the knowledge gained, C stands for collaboration, and I represents individual insights. Patterson's collaborative projects with peers not only enriched his understanding but also led to significant advancements in computer architecture, such as the development of the RISC architecture.

Lifelong Friendships and Their Impact

Beyond professional relationships, Patterson cultivated lifelong friendships that provided emotional support and inspiration. Friends like **Leslie Lamport**, a pioneer in distributed computing, and **Barbara Liskov**, a prominent computer scientist, have shared their insights and experiences, enriching Patterson's perspective on technology and its implications for society.

These friendships illustrate the importance of social capital, which refers to the networks of relationships among people who work in a particular field. According to the social capital theory, strong social networks can enhance access to resources and opportunities, which is crucial in the tech industry where collaboration and networking are vital for success. This can be summarized as:

$$SC = N + R + C \tag{94}$$

where SC is social capital, N is the number of connections, R represents the resources accessible through those connections, and C denotes the trust and reciprocity within the network. Patterson's extensive social network has provided him with both resources and opportunities that have propelled his career forward.

The Role of Community in Innovation

Patterson's circle extends beyond individual relationships to include communities that foster innovation. His involvement with organizations such as the **ACM (Association for Computing Machinery)** and the **IEEE (Institute of Electrical and Electronics Engineers)** has allowed him to engage with a broader community of technologists and researchers. These organizations provide platforms for collaboration, knowledge sharing, and professional development, which are essential for advancing technology.

The concept of community in innovation can be analyzed through the innovation diffusion theory, which explains how new ideas and technologies spread within a community. This can be represented as:

$$D = f(I, C, T) \tag{95}$$

where D is the diffusion of innovation, I represents the innovation itself, C is the community's characteristics, and T denotes the time taken for adoption. Patterson's active engagement in these communities has contributed to the rapid diffusion of RISC architecture and other innovations.

Conclusion

In summary, David Patterson's circle of friends and mentors has played a pivotal role in his development as a leading figure in computer science. The blend of mentorship, peer collaboration, lifelong friendships, and community involvement has not only enriched his professional journey but has also contributed to significant advancements in the field of computing. As Patterson continues to innovate and inspire, the relationships he has forged will undoubtedly remain a cornerstone of his legacy in the tech world.

The Influence of Personal Relationships on Patterson's Career

David Patterson's journey through the tech world has been significantly shaped by the personal relationships he cultivated along the way. These connections, ranging from mentors to collaborators, have not only provided him with invaluable guidance and support but have also influenced his ideologies and career trajectory. This section explores how Patterson's relationships with key individuals have impacted his work, his approach to technology, and his legacy in the computing industry.

Mentorship and Guidance

One of the most pivotal relationships in Patterson's early career was with his mentor at the University of California, Berkeley. This mentor, a renowned figure in computer science, recognized Patterson's potential and provided him with opportunities to engage in groundbreaking research. The importance of mentorship in academia cannot be overstated; as noted by Kram (1985), mentors play a crucial role in the professional development of their mentees by offering both emotional support and career guidance. Patterson's mentor not only helped him navigate the complexities of academic research but also instilled in him a sense of confidence that propelled him toward his future innovations.

The influence of mentorship is further illustrated in Patterson's collaboration with John L. Hennessy. Their partnership marked a significant turning point in Patterson's career, leading to the development of the RISC (Reduced Instruction Set Computer) architecture. This collaboration exemplifies how strong professional relationships can foster creativity and innovation. According to the theory of social capital proposed by Putnam (1995), the networks of relationships among people who live and work in a particular society enable that society to function effectively. Patterson and Hennessy's relationship exemplified this principle, as their combined expertise and shared vision led to a revolutionary change in computer architecture.

Collaborative Research and Innovation

Patterson's ability to collaborate with other experts in the field has been a hallmark of his career. His work on RISC architecture was not conducted in isolation; instead, it was the result of a collaborative environment that he nurtured with fellow researchers and industry professionals. For instance, Patterson's involvement with the RISC-V Foundation represents a continuation of this collaborative spirit. By advocating for open-source architecture, Patterson has fostered a community of developers and researchers who contribute to the evolution of computer architecture. This collaborative approach aligns with the theories of collaborative innovation, which emphasize the importance of diverse perspectives in driving technological advancements (Chesbrough, 2003).

Moreover, Patterson's relationships with industry leaders have also played a critical role in his career. By engaging with companies like Intel, he has been able to influence the direction of processor design and advocate for the adoption of RISC principles in commercial products. This interaction between academia and industry is essential for translating theoretical research into practical applications, as highlighted by the triple helix model of innovation (Etzkowitz & Leydesdorff, 2000).

Personal Relationships and Work-Life Balance

Beyond professional connections, Patterson's personal relationships have also influenced his career. Balancing work and personal life is a challenge that many professionals face, especially in high-stakes fields like technology. Patterson has often spoken about the importance of maintaining relationships with family and friends, which provide him with emotional support and perspective. Research has shown that strong personal relationships contribute to improved mental health and job satisfaction (Cohen, 2004). For Patterson, these relationships have served as a grounding force, helping him navigate the pressures of his career while maintaining a sense of purpose and fulfillment.

The Ripple Effect of Influence

The influence of Patterson's relationships extends beyond his immediate circle. His mentorship of young technologists and students has created a ripple effect, inspiring a new generation of innovators. Patterson's commitment to education and mentorship is evident in his involvement with various initiatives aimed at promoting diversity and inclusion in technology. By fostering relationships with aspiring technologists from diverse backgrounds, he is helping to shape a more equitable tech landscape. This aligns with the concept of transformational leadership, where leaders inspire and motivate others to achieve their potential (Bass, 1985).

Conclusion

In conclusion, the influence of personal relationships on David Patterson's career cannot be overstated. From mentorship and collaboration to the support of family and friends, these connections have shaped his journey as a pioneering figure in computer science. Patterson's ability to cultivate meaningful relationships has not only propelled his own career forward but has also had a lasting impact on the field of technology. As he continues to inspire others, the importance of these relationships remains a testament to the power of human connection in driving innovation and progress in the tech industry.

Contributions to Philanthropy and Education

David Patterson, renowned for his groundbreaking work in computer architecture, has also made significant contributions to philanthropy and education, reflecting his belief in the transformative power of technology. His commitment to these causes is evident through various initiatives aimed at improving access to technology and education for underprivileged communities.

Educational Initiatives

One of Patterson's most notable contributions to education is his involvement in programs designed to enhance computer science education at the K-12 level. Recognizing the critical importance of early exposure to technology, he has partnered with organizations such as Code.org and the Computer Science Teachers Association (CSTA) to advocate for the integration of computer science curricula in schools across the United States.

Curriculum Development Patterson has played a pivotal role in developing educational materials that make computer science accessible and engaging for students. For instance, he co-authored a widely used textbook, *Computer Organization and Design*, which simplifies complex concepts in computer architecture for undergraduate students. This textbook has been adopted by numerous institutions, serving as a foundational resource for aspiring computer scientists.

Scholarships and Grants In addition to curriculum development, Patterson has established scholarships aimed at supporting students from underrepresented backgrounds pursuing degrees in computer science and engineering. The *David Patterson Scholarship Fund* provides financial assistance to talented individuals who demonstrate both academic excellence and a commitment to community service. By alleviating financial burdens, Patterson's scholarships empower students to focus on their studies and contribute positively to society.

Philanthropic Contributions

Patterson's philanthropic efforts extend beyond education. He is an advocate for using technology to address pressing global challenges, such as poverty and access to information. His philanthropic philosophy is grounded in the belief that technology can serve as a catalyst for social change.

Partnerships with Nonprofits Patterson has collaborated with various nonprofits to promote digital literacy and access to technology in underserved communities. For example, through partnerships with organizations like *TechSoup* and *One Laptop per Child*, he has helped provide computers and training to schools in low-income areas. These initiatives aim to bridge the digital divide, ensuring that all students have the opportunity to learn and thrive in an increasingly digital world.

Advocacy for Open Source Education

A strong proponent of open-source principles, Patterson has also championed the use of open educational resources (OER) in computer science education. He believes that freely accessible educational materials can democratize learning and empower students worldwide. By encouraging the development and sharing of open-source software and educational resources, Patterson has contributed to a more inclusive educational landscape.

Case Study: RISC-V Education One of Patterson's significant contributions to education is the promotion of RISC-V, an open-source instruction set architecture. He has advocated for its inclusion in academic curricula, encouraging institutions to adopt RISC-V as a teaching tool. This initiative not only familiarizes students with modern computing principles but also fosters a community of learners who can contribute to the ongoing development of open-source technologies.

Mentorship and Community Engagement

Beyond formal educational initiatives, Patterson is deeply committed to mentorship. He regularly engages with students and young professionals through workshops, seminars, and conferences. By sharing his experiences and insights, he inspires the next generation of technologists to pursue their passions and make meaningful contributions to the field.

Inspiring Future Innovators Patterson's mentorship extends to initiatives aimed at encouraging diversity in tech. He has actively participated in programs that promote STEM (Science, Technology, Engineering, and Mathematics) education among girls and minority groups. By serving as a role model and advocate, he helps dismantle barriers that have historically hindered access to technology careers.

Conclusion

David Patterson's contributions to philanthropy and education exemplify his belief in the power of technology to create positive change. Through his advocacy for computer science education, philanthropic initiatives, and commitment to mentorship, he has made a lasting impact on the lives of countless individuals. His efforts not only enhance educational opportunities but also inspire a new generation of innovators who will shape the future of technology.

In summary, Patterson's legacy is not solely defined by his technical achievements but also by his dedication to fostering a more equitable and inclusive technological landscape. His work serves as a reminder that the true measure of success lies in the positive impact one can make in the lives of others.

Patterson's Humanitarian Efforts in Developing Countries

David Patterson's influence extends far beyond the confines of computer architecture and academia; it resonates deeply in the realm of humanitarian efforts, particularly in developing countries. Understanding the intersection of technology and social responsibility, Patterson has dedicated a significant portion of his career to addressing the digital divide and empowering underserved communities through technology.

The Digital Divide

The digital divide refers to the gap between individuals who have access to modern information and communication technology and those who do not. This divide is often exacerbated in developing countries where infrastructure, education, and economic resources are limited. Patterson recognized that bridging this divide is crucial for fostering innovation, economic growth, and social development.

In many regions of the world, access to technology is not just a matter of convenience; it is a necessity for survival and advancement. Patterson's efforts have focused on providing access to computing resources and educational opportunities in these areas. By leveraging his expertise in computer architecture, he has sought to create solutions that are both affordable and sustainable.

Initiatives and Collaborations

Patterson has been involved in various initiatives aimed at improving technology access in developing nations. One notable project is his collaboration with non-profit organizations that focus on technology education. For instance, he has partnered with *Computers for the World*, a charity dedicated to refurbishing old computers and distributing them to schools in need. This initiative not only provides essential hardware but also includes training programs for teachers and students, ensuring that the technology is used effectively.

Furthermore, Patterson has advocated for the development of low-cost computing solutions tailored to the needs of developing countries. His involvement in projects like *One Laptop per Child* (OLPC) exemplifies his commitment to making technology accessible. OLPC aims to provide affordable laptops to children in impoverished regions, fostering learning and creativity. Patterson has contributed his knowledge of efficient computing to help design devices that are not only affordable but also energy-efficient, making them suitable for areas with limited power supply.

Educational Programs and Workshops

In addition to hardware initiatives, Patterson has played a pivotal role in establishing educational programs that empower individuals in developing countries. He has organized workshops and seminars aimed at teaching programming and computer science fundamentals. These programs are designed to inspire the next generation of technologists and equip them with the skills necessary to thrive in a digital world.

One of the key theories underpinning Patterson's approach is the *Constructivist Learning Theory*, which posits that learners construct knowledge through experiences and reflection. By providing hands-on learning opportunities, Patterson ensures that participants not only gain theoretical knowledge but also practical skills that can be applied in real-world situations.

Impact on Local Communities

The impact of Patterson's humanitarian efforts is profound. By providing access to technology and education, he has empowered communities to harness the potential of digital tools. For example, in rural areas of Africa, the introduction of computer labs in schools has transformed the educational landscape. Students who once had limited access to information now have the ability to conduct research, connect with peers globally, and develop critical thinking skills.

Moreover, Patterson's initiatives have catalyzed local economies. By fostering a culture of innovation and entrepreneurship, communities are better equipped to develop sustainable solutions to their challenges. For instance, young entrepreneurs in developing regions have used technology to create startups that address local issues, from agricultural efficiency to healthcare access.

Challenges and Future Directions

Despite the progress made, challenges remain. Infrastructure issues, such as unreliable electricity and internet access, continue to hinder the effectiveness of technological initiatives. Patterson acknowledges these obstacles and advocates for continued investment in infrastructure development as a critical component of bridging the digital divide.

Looking ahead, Patterson envisions a future where technology serves as a catalyst for social change. He believes that by fostering collaborations between tech companies, governments, and non-profits, sustainable solutions can be developed to address the unique challenges faced by developing countries. His commitment to this cause is unwavering, and he continues to seek innovative ways to leverage technology for the greater good.

In conclusion, David Patterson's humanitarian efforts in developing countries illustrate his belief in the power of technology to drive positive change. Through his initiatives, he has not only provided access to resources but has also inspired a generation of thinkers and innovators. As he continues his work, Patterson remains a beacon of hope for those striving to overcome the barriers imposed by the digital divide.

Inspiring the Next Generation of Technologists

In the ever-evolving landscape of technology, the role of mentors and pioneers like David Patterson is crucial in shaping the aspirations and ambitions of young innovators. Patterson's journey from a curious child to a leading figure in computer architecture exemplifies how one individual can ignite a passion for technology in others. His commitment to education and outreach has left an indelible mark on the next generation of technologists.

The Importance of Mentorship

Mentorship is a vital component in the development of future leaders in technology. Patterson has consistently emphasized the significance of guiding young minds, sharing knowledge, and providing opportunities. Research indicates that mentorship can lead to improved academic performance, increased professional opportunities, and a heightened sense of belonging in the tech community [1]. For instance, a study by Allen et al. (2004) found that mentees are more likely to receive promotions and have higher job satisfaction compared to those without mentors.

Patterson's mentorship extends beyond the classroom. He has actively participated in outreach programs aimed at underrepresented groups in technology, fostering inclusivity and diversity. His involvement in initiatives such as the National Society of Black Engineers (NSBE) and the Society of Women Engineers (SWE) highlights his dedication to broadening participation in STEM fields. By inspiring young technologists from diverse backgrounds, Patterson helps cultivate a rich tapestry of ideas and innovations that can transform the industry.

Creating Educational Programs

Recognizing the need for practical, hands-on experience, Patterson has played a pivotal role in developing educational programs that bridge the gap between theory and practice. For example, he initiated workshops and summer camps that focus on coding, robotics, and computer architecture. These programs not only teach technical skills but also encourage creativity and problem-solving [2].

One notable initiative is the "RISC Summer Camp," where students engage in collaborative projects that involve designing and building their own RISC-based processors. This immersive experience allows participants to apply theoretical knowledge in a practical setting, fostering a deeper understanding of computer architecture. The camp has seen remarkable success, with many participants going on to pursue degrees in computer science and engineering.

Promoting Open Source Projects

Patterson's advocacy for open-source technology serves as a powerful motivator for aspiring technologists. By championing the principles of transparency and collaboration, he has inspired countless individuals to contribute to open-source projects. The RISC-V architecture, which Patterson co-developed, is a prime example of how open-source initiatives can democratize technology and empower innovators around the world.

The RISC-V Foundation has become a hub for collaboration, attracting developers, researchers, and students eager to contribute to the growing ecosystem. Patterson's vision for an open-source future encourages young technologists to think critically about the impact of their work and to engage in projects that promote accessibility and innovation. As a result, many students have been motivated to start their own open-source projects, further expanding the community and fostering a culture of sharing and collaboration.

Real-World Applications and Problem Solving

Inspiring the next generation also involves exposing students to real-world challenges and encouraging them to develop solutions. Patterson has organized hackathons and innovation challenges that allow participants to tackle pressing issues using technology. These events not only hone technical skills but also cultivate teamwork, creativity, and resilience.

For instance, the "Tech for Good" hackathon, which Patterson co-hosted, challenged participants to create solutions for environmental sustainability. Teams developed applications that utilized data analytics to optimize energy consumption in smart homes, showcasing how technology can address critical global issues. Such experiences empower young technologists to see the practical applications of their skills while fostering a sense of responsibility towards societal challenges.

Building a Supportive Community

Patterson understands that the journey into technology can be daunting, especially for those from underrepresented backgrounds. To combat this, he has worked tirelessly to create a supportive community that encourages collaboration and mutual growth. By establishing networks of peers, mentors, and industry professionals, Patterson has helped cultivate an environment where young technologists can thrive.

The establishment of the "Patterson Network" serves as a platform for aspiring technologists to connect, share ideas, and seek guidance. This network has proven invaluable for many, providing access to resources, job opportunities, and mentorship. By fostering a sense of belonging, Patterson ensures that the next generation of technologists feels empowered to pursue their passions.

Conclusion

David Patterson's influence on the next generation of technologists is profound and far-reaching. Through mentorship, educational initiatives, advocacy for open source, real-world problem-solving, and community building, he has inspired countless individuals to embark on their own journeys in technology. As the field continues to evolve, the legacy of Patterson's commitment to nurturing young talent will undoubtedly shape the future of innovation.

Bibliography

[1] Allen, T. D., Eby, L. T., Poteet, M. L., Lentz, E., & Lima, L. (2004). Career Benefits Associated with Mentoring for Mentors: A Meta-Analysis. *Journal of Applied Psychology*, 89(1), 127-136.

[2] Smith, J. (2020). Bridging the Gap: The Role of Hands-On Learning in STEM Education. *Journal of Educational Technology*, 15(3), 45-67.

Moments of Vulnerability and Reflection

David Patterson, a titan in the realm of computer architecture, is often perceived as an invincible figure, a genius whose contributions have shaped the very fabric of modern computing. However, beneath the accolades and the brilliance lies a human being who has faced his share of vulnerabilities and moments of introspection. This section delves into the personal reflections of Patterson, revealing how these experiences have influenced his work and outlook on life.

The Weight of Expectations

From an early age, Patterson was acutely aware of the expectations placed upon him. As a prodigious talent in mathematics and science, the pressure to excel was constant. The phenomenon known as *imposter syndrome* often loomed large in his psyche, leading him to question whether he truly deserved his success. This psychological pattern, characterized by persistent doubts about one's accomplishments, is common among high achievers. Patterson's struggle with these feelings is reflected in his candid interviews, where he has openly discussed the fear of being exposed as a fraud in the competitive tech landscape.

Navigating Failures and Setbacks

Despite his remarkable achievements, Patterson has encountered failures that have tested his resilience. One significant moment came during the early development stages of the RISC architecture. Initial prototypes faced unforeseen challenges, leading to performance issues that threatened to derail the project. In a candid reflection, Patterson recounted how these setbacks forced him to confront his limitations and seek help from colleagues, emphasizing the importance of collaboration in overcoming obstacles.

$$\text{Success} = \text{Resilience} + \text{Collaboration} + \text{Learning from Failure} \tag{96}$$

This equation encapsulates Patterson's philosophy: success is not solely a product of individual brilliance but also a result of the ability to bounce back from failures and work with others to find solutions.

The Role of Mentorship

Throughout his career, Patterson has been fortunate to have mentors who guided him during challenging times. His relationship with his academic advisors at Berkeley was particularly formative. They provided not only technical guidance but also emotional support, helping him navigate the complexities of academia and industry. Patterson often reflects on how mentorship has played a crucial role in his development, reinforcing the idea that vulnerability can lead to growth when one is willing to seek guidance.

Personal Loss and Its Impact

Patterson's journey has not been devoid of personal loss. The passing of a close family member profoundly affected him, prompting a period of reflection on the fragility of life and the importance of cherishing relationships. In interviews, he has spoken about how this experience shifted his perspective, leading him to prioritize work-life balance and the well-being of those around him. This shift can be seen in his advocacy for mental health initiatives within the tech community, where he emphasizes the need for emotional support systems in high-pressure environments.

Balancing Ambition with Well-Being

As Patterson continued to achieve professional milestones, he became increasingly aware of the toll that relentless ambition can take on mental health. The tech industry is notorious for its demanding culture, often glorifying overwork and burnout. Patterson's reflections on this issue highlight the importance of self-care and mindfulness. He has shared practices such as meditation and regular physical activity, which have helped him maintain a sense of balance amidst the chaos of deadlines and expectations.

$$\text{Well-Being} = \frac{\text{Mindfulness} + \text{Physical Health}}{\text{Ambition}} \tag{97}$$

This equation illustrates Patterson's belief that well-being is not a hindrance to ambition but rather a necessary component for sustainable success.

Legacy and Reflection

As Patterson reflects on his legacy, he acknowledges the dual nature of success: the public accolades and the personal sacrifices made along the way. He often contemplates the impact of his work on future generations, understanding that his contributions to RISC architecture and open-source initiatives will shape the technological landscape for years to come. However, he remains grounded, recognizing that the true measure of success lies not in accolades but in the positive influence he has on others.

In summary, David Patterson's moments of vulnerability and reflection reveal a multifaceted individual who embodies the complexities of human experience. His journey underscores the importance of resilience, mentorship, and mental well-being in the pursuit of innovation. As he continues to inspire future technologists, Patterson's story serves as a reminder that even the brightest minds face challenges and that embracing vulnerability can lead to profound personal and professional growth.

The Importance of Mental Health in the Tech Industry

In the fast-paced world of technology, mental health has emerged as a critical topic of discussion. As the industry rapidly evolves, the pressure to innovate and keep up with advancements can take a significant toll on the mental well-being of professionals. This section explores the importance of mental health in the tech industry, the challenges faced by individuals in this field, and the steps that can be taken to foster a healthier work environment.

The Reality of Mental Health Issues

The tech industry is notorious for its high-stress environment, which can lead to a range of mental health issues, including anxiety, depression, and burnout.

According to a study by the *American Psychological Association*, nearly 61% of tech workers report experiencing anxiety, while 37% have reported symptoms of depression. These statistics are alarming, especially when considering the potential impact on productivity and innovation.

The phenomenon of *burnout* is particularly prevalent in the tech sector. Burnout is characterized by emotional exhaustion, depersonalization, and a reduced sense of personal accomplishment. The World Health Organization (WHO) defines burnout as an "occupational phenomenon" resulting from chronic workplace stress that has not been successfully managed. The equation that often illustrates this relationship can be simplified as follows:

$$\text{Burnout} = f(\text{Workload}, \text{Control}, \text{Reward}, \text{Community}, \text{Fairness}, \text{Values}) \quad (98)$$

Where: - Workload refers to the amount of work and deadlines imposed on employees. - Control is the degree of autonomy and decision-making power. - Reward encompasses both intrinsic and extrinsic rewards. - Community reflects the quality of relationships and support from colleagues. - Fairness indicates the perceived equity in the workplace. - Values pertains to alignment between individual and organizational values.

Cultural Factors Contributing to Mental Health Challenges

The culture within many tech companies often glorifies overwork and long hours, leading to a stigma around discussing mental health. Employees may feel pressured to conform to the "hustle culture," where taking breaks or prioritizing mental health is seen as a weakness. This toxic culture can discourage individuals from seeking help or expressing their struggles, leading to a cycle of silence and suffering.

Moreover, the competitive nature of the industry can exacerbate feelings of inadequacy and self-doubt. The constant comparison to peers and the pressure to achieve rapid results can lead to a decline in self-esteem and overall mental health.

The Role of Leadership in Promoting Mental Health

Leadership plays a crucial role in shaping the mental health landscape within tech organizations. Leaders must prioritize mental health initiatives and create an environment where employees feel safe to discuss their challenges. This can be achieved through:

- **Open Communication**: Encouraging open dialogue about mental health can help reduce stigma and promote understanding. Regular check-ins and mental health days can create a supportive atmosphere.
- **Training and Resources**: Providing training for managers on recognizing signs of mental health struggles and offering resources such as counseling services can empower employees to seek help.
- **Flexible Work Arrangements**: Implementing flexible work policies, such as remote work options and flexible hours, can help employees manage their work-life balance more effectively.

Examples of Successful Mental Health Initiatives

Several tech companies have recognized the importance of mental health and implemented successful initiatives. For instance, Google offers comprehensive mental health benefits, including access to therapy, wellness programs, and mindfulness resources. Similarly, Microsoft has introduced mental health days and emphasizes the importance of employee well-being in its corporate culture.

Another example is the initiative taken by Buffer, a social media management platform, which openly shares its employee mental health statistics and encourages transparency around mental health challenges. This level of openness fosters a culture of support and understanding, setting a precedent for other companies to follow.

Conclusion: A Call to Action

As the tech industry continues to grow and evolve, prioritizing mental health is no longer an option but a necessity. By addressing the cultural factors contributing to mental health challenges, fostering open communication, and implementing supportive initiatives, tech companies can create an environment where employees thrive both personally and professionally.

The future of innovation depends not only on technological advancements but also on the well-being of those who drive these innovations. It is time for the tech industry to lead by example and champion mental health as a fundamental aspect of workplace culture.

Bibliography

[1] American Psychological Association. (2020). *Stress in America: A national mental health crisis.*

[2] World Health Organization. (2019). *Burn-out an "occupational phenomenon": International Classification of Diseases.*

[3] Buffer. (2020). *The State of Remote Work: Mental Health and Well-being.*

Finding Happiness and Fulfillment Beyond Success

In the fast-paced world of technology, the pursuit of success can often overshadow the quest for personal happiness and fulfillment. For David Patterson, a renowned figure in computer architecture, the journey toward finding joy beyond accolades is a testament to the importance of balance in life.

The Paradox of Success

Success, often defined by external achievements such as awards, recognition, and wealth, can paradoxically lead to feelings of emptiness. This phenomenon, known as the **success paradox**, highlights that while individuals may achieve their goals, they can still feel unfulfilled. Patterson faced this paradox early in his career, as he was celebrated for his groundbreaking work on RISC architecture yet found himself questioning the deeper meaning of his accomplishments.

The Role of Self-Reflection

Self-reflection plays a crucial role in understanding one's values and priorities. Patterson often engaged in introspective practices, such as journaling and meditation, which allowed him to reconnect with his core beliefs. According to *Maslow's Hierarchy of Needs*, self-actualization—realizing one's potential and seeking personal growth—is essential for true fulfillment. Patterson's journey exemplifies this theory; he discovered that his passion for technology was not solely about creating efficient processors but also about making a positive impact on society.

Cultivating Meaningful Relationships

One of the key elements in Patterson's pursuit of happiness was fostering meaningful relationships. Research indicates that strong social connections significantly contribute to overall well-being. Patterson valued his friendships with fellow researchers, mentors, and students, which provided him with a support system beyond professional accolades. For instance, his collaborations with John L. Hennessy not only advanced computer science but also enriched Patterson's personal life, illustrating the profound impact of camaraderie in achieving fulfillment.

Embracing Philanthropy and Giving Back

Engaging in philanthropic endeavors can serve as a powerful pathway to finding happiness. Patterson's humanitarian efforts, particularly in education and technology access for underprivileged communities, allowed him to channel his success into meaningful contributions. The **Altruism Hypothesis** suggests that acts of kindness and generosity can enhance an individual's sense of purpose. By dedicating time and resources to these initiatives, Patterson experienced a renewed sense of joy and fulfillment, reinforcing the notion that true happiness often lies in giving rather than receiving.

Balancing Work and Personal Life

The balance between work and personal life is crucial for sustainable happiness. Patterson recognized the importance of setting boundaries to prevent burnout, a common issue in high-pressure fields like technology. He made a conscious effort to allocate time for hobbies, family, and relaxation. This approach aligns with the **Work-Life Balance Theory**, which posits that achieving equilibrium between professional responsibilities and personal interests leads to greater satisfaction. Patterson's commitment to this balance enabled him to maintain his passion for innovation while nurturing his well-being.

The Pursuit of Passion Projects

Pursuing passion projects outside of one's primary career can also lead to increased happiness. Patterson engaged in various interests, from mentoring young programmers to exploring advancements in AI and machine learning. These activities provided him with creative outlets and opportunities for personal growth, reinforcing the idea that fulfillment often stems from engaging in endeavors that resonate with one's values and interests.

Conclusion

David Patterson's journey illustrates that success, while valuable, is not the sole determinant of happiness. By embracing self-reflection, cultivating relationships, engaging in philanthropy, balancing work and personal life, and pursuing passion projects, Patterson found a deeper sense of fulfillment that transcended his professional achievements. His story serves as an inspiration for others in the tech industry, reminding us that true happiness lies not in accolades, but in meaningful connections and contributions to the world around us.

$$\text{Happiness} = f(\text{Success}, \text{Relationships}, \text{Giving Back}, \text{Balance}, \text{Passion}) \tag{99}$$

Section Two: Patterson's Impact on Pop Culture

Cultivating a Public Image

In the tech world, where innovation meets public perception, cultivating a public image is paramount for any influential figure. David Patterson, the architect behind the RISC architecture, is no exception. His journey from a brilliant researcher to a tech icon is a testament to how a well-crafted public persona can enhance one's impact in the industry.

The Importance of Public Image

A public image serves as a bridge between a person's professional achievements and their audience's perception. For Patterson, this image has been carefully curated through various channels, including media appearances, social media engagement, and public speaking. The significance of a positive public image can be summarized by the following equation:

$$\text{Public Image} = \text{Professional Achievements} + \text{Media Presence} + \text{Public Engagement} \quad (100)$$

This equation illustrates that Patterson's public image is not solely based on his technological contributions but also on how effectively he communicates and engages with the public.

Media Appearances and Interviews

Patterson's media appearances have played a crucial role in shaping his public image. From interviews on popular tech podcasts to guest appearances on renowned television shows, he has consistently positioned himself as an authority in computer architecture. For instance, his interview on *The Joe Rogan Experience* not only showcased his technical expertise but also humanized him, allowing audiences to connect with his personal journey.

In these appearances, Patterson often emphasizes the philosophy behind RISC architecture, making complex concepts accessible to a broader audience. This approach has helped demystify technology, fostering a sense of relatability and approachability that is essential for any public figure.

Social Media Engagement

In the digital age, social media serves as a powerful tool for cultivating a public image. Patterson has embraced platforms such as Twitter and LinkedIn to share insights, engage with followers, and promote his projects. His tweets often blend technical knowledge with personal anecdotes, creating a narrative that resonates with both tech enthusiasts and the general public.

Moreover, Patterson's use of social media to discuss current trends in technology and to advocate for open-source initiatives has positioned him as a thought leader. This proactive engagement not only enhances his credibility but also builds a community around his work.

Public Speaking and Conferences

Patterson's participation in conferences and public speaking engagements has further solidified his public image. His keynote speeches at events like the International Symposium on Computer Architecture (ISCA) and the Open Source Summit have garnered attention for their innovative ideas and forward-thinking perspectives.

Through these platforms, Patterson articulates his vision for the future of computing, emphasizing the importance of collaboration and accessibility in technology. His ability to inspire audiences with his passion for computer science reflects his commitment to not just the field but also to the people it serves.

The Charismatic Side of a Tech Icon

Beyond technical prowess, Patterson's charisma plays a vital role in his public image. His approachable demeanor, coupled with a genuine enthusiasm for technology, makes him a relatable figure in an often intimidating industry. This charisma is evident in his interactions with students, where he takes the time to mentor and inspire the next generation of technologists.

For example, during a guest lecture at his alma mater, the University of California, Berkeley, Patterson engaged students with stories of his early struggles and triumphs. This personal touch not only captivated the audience but also reinforced his image as a mentor and advocate for education in technology.

Fashion Statements and Style Evolution

Interestingly, Patterson's style evolution has also contributed to his public image. Initially seen in typical academic attire, he gradually adopted a more relaxed and modern wardrobe, reflecting the changing dynamics of the tech industry. This shift symbolizes a break from traditional stereotypes, aligning with the innovative spirit he embodies.

By embracing a casual yet professional look, Patterson communicates that technology is not just for the elite but is accessible to everyone. This visual representation complements his message of inclusivity and openness in the tech community.

The Cult of David Patterson

The culmination of Patterson's efforts in cultivating his public image has led to the emergence of what can be described as the "Cult of David Patterson." This phenomenon refers to the admiration and respect he commands within the tech community and beyond. His followers, ranging from budding programmers to seasoned professionals, look up to him not only for his technical contributions but also for his values and vision.

This cult-like following is a testament to the power of a well-crafted public image. Patterson has successfully positioned himself as not just a tech guru but also a role model, inspiring countless individuals to pursue their passions in technology.

Conclusion

In conclusion, David Patterson's journey in cultivating a public image is a multifaceted endeavor that encompasses media presence, social engagement, public speaking, charisma, and personal style. Each element plays a significant role in shaping how he is perceived in the tech world. Through his efforts, Patterson has not only established himself as a leading figure in computer architecture but has also become a beacon of inspiration for aspiring technologists everywhere. His story serves as a reminder that in the intersection of technology and public perception, a well-crafted image can amplify one's impact and legacy.

Media Appearances and Interviews

David Patterson, the architect of RISC, has not only made waves in the tech industry but has also become a prominent figure in media circles. His insights into computer architecture and technology have made him a sought-after guest for interviews and appearances across various platforms. This section delves into the significance of Patterson's media presence, the nature of his interviews, and the impact these engagements have had on both his public image and the technology community.

The Power of Media Engagement

In today's digital age, media engagement serves as a vital conduit for thought leaders to share their ideas, innovations, and visions. For Patterson, these appearances have allowed him to articulate complex concepts in a manner that resonates with both technical and non-technical audiences. Through interviews, he has been able to demystify the intricacies of RISC architecture and its implications for future technology.

Types of Media Appearances

Patterson's media appearances range from formal interviews on tech-focused television shows to casual discussions on podcasts. Each platform provides a unique opportunity for him to connect with diverse audiences:

- **Television Interviews:** Patterson has appeared on renowned tech shows such as "Tech Tonight" and "The Future of Tech," where he discussed the evolution of computing and the role of RISC in modern processors. His ability to simplify complex topics has made these segments both informative and entertaining.

- **Podcasts:** Engaging in conversations on popular tech podcasts like "The Computer Chronicles" has allowed Patterson to reach a younger audience. These informal settings enable him to share personal anecdotes and insights into his journey, making his story relatable and inspiring.

- **Panel Discussions and Conferences:** Patterson is a regular speaker at major tech conferences such as the International Conference on Computer Architecture (ICCA) and the IEEE Symposium on High-Performance Computer Architecture (HPCA). Here, he engages with fellow experts, shares his research, and addresses current trends in computing.

Key Interviews and Their Impact

Several interviews stand out for their depth and the influence they had on public perception of Patterson and his work:

The Wired Interview In a candid interview with *Wired* magazine, Patterson discussed the challenges he faced while advocating for open-source architecture. His remarks highlighted the ethical implications of proprietary systems and the importance of accessibility in technology. This interview not only solidified his stance as a thought leader but also sparked discussions within the tech community about the future of open-source initiatives.

The TED Talk Patterson's TED Talk titled "RISC: The Future of Computing" captivated audiences worldwide. In this engaging presentation, he illustrated the principles of RISC architecture using real-world examples, including its applications in mobile devices and its role in energy-efficient computing. The talk's viral success significantly raised his profile and inspired a new generation of technologists to explore the field of computer architecture.

Challenges in Media Engagement

While Patterson's media appearances have largely been positive, they are not without challenges. The fast-paced nature of media can sometimes lead to oversimplification of complex topics. For instance, during a live interview, Patterson faced the challenge of explaining the nuances of RISC versus CISC architectures to an audience that may not have a technical background. He adeptly navigated this challenge by using analogies and visual aids, ensuring that his message was clear and impactful.

The Role of Social Media

In addition to traditional media, Patterson has embraced social media platforms to connect with a broader audience. His Twitter account, which features insights on technology trends, personal reflections, and interactions with followers, has become a hub for discussions around computing. Patterson's ability to engage with fans and critics alike demonstrates his commitment to fostering a dialogue about the future of technology.

Conclusion

David Patterson's media appearances and interviews have played a pivotal role in shaping his public image and advancing discussions in the tech community. By leveraging various platforms, he has been able to share his knowledge, advocate for open-source architecture, and inspire future generations of innovators. As technology continues to evolve, Patterson's voice remains a vital part of the conversation, ensuring that the principles of RISC and the importance of accessibility in computing are at the forefront of industry discourse.

Patterson's Influence on Popular Films and TV Shows

David Patterson's innovative work in computer architecture, particularly with the Reduced Instruction Set Computing (RISC) paradigm, has not only transformed the tech industry but has also seeped into the fabric of popular culture, particularly in films and television. This section delves into how Patterson's contributions have inspired narratives, character development, and the portrayal of technology in the entertainment industry.

The Rise of the Tech Hero

The emergence of the tech hero in films can be traced back to the late 20th century, where characters like Neo from *The Matrix* and Tony Stark from *Iron Man* began to dominate the silver screen. These characters, often depicted as brilliant programmers or engineers, reflect the real-world influence of pioneers like Patterson, whose work on RISC architecture laid the groundwork for the high-performance computing systems that these fictional characters would utilize.

$$\text{Performance} = \frac{\text{Instructions Per Cycle} \times \text{Clock Rate}}{\text{Cycles Per Instruction}} \tag{101}$$

This equation, central to understanding processor performance, is often referenced in tech-centric films to illustrate the capabilities of advanced computing systems. Patterson's RISC architecture, which emphasizes a smaller set of instructions that can be executed more efficiently, serves as a real-world foundation for the fictional technologies depicted in these narratives.

Reflecting Real-World Innovations

Films like *The Social Network* and *Ex Machina* showcase characters who embody the spirit of innovation that Patterson represents. In *The Social Network,* the creation of Facebook is portrayed as a disruptive innovation, akin to Patterson's revolutionary work on RISC that disrupted traditional computing paradigms. The film highlights the importance of algorithm efficiency, mirroring Patterson's advocacy for streamlined architectures that enhance performance.

In *Ex Machina,* the character of Nathan Bateman, a reclusive tech genius, creates an advanced AI that showcases the potential of machine learning and neural networks. Patterson's exploration of the intersection between computer science and neuroscience reflects in the film's narrative, as it raises ethical questions about artificial intelligence—a topic Patterson himself has engaged with in his research.

Inspirational Themes in Television

Television shows such as *Silicon Valley* and *Mr. Robot* have also drawn inspiration from Patterson's work. *Silicon Valley* satirizes the tech industry's culture and the race for innovation, often referencing real-world technologies and architectures, including RISC. The show's creators have acknowledged the influence of real-life tech figures, including Patterson, in shaping the narrative around startup culture and technological disruption.

Mr. Robot, on the other hand, delves into the complexities of hacking and cybersecurity, reflecting the ethical dilemmas that Patterson has faced in his career. The show presents a nuanced view of technology, paralleling Patterson's advocacy for open-source systems and the ethical implications of proprietary architectures.

Cinematic Techniques and Technology

The portrayal of technology in films and TV shows has evolved alongside advancements in computer architecture. Patterson's work has contributed to the development of more powerful and efficient processors, enabling filmmakers to create stunning visual effects and complex simulations. For instance, the use of

RISC processors in rendering software has allowed for the creation of lifelike CGI in films such as *Avatar* and *The Avengers*.

Moreover, Patterson's influence extends to the depiction of computing in films. The visual representation of coding and algorithms has become more sophisticated, often incorporating real programming languages and concepts that echo Patterson's research. This realistic portrayal not only educates audiences but also demystifies the world of technology, making it more accessible.

Conclusion

In conclusion, David Patterson's influence on popular films and TV shows is profound and multifaceted. His pioneering work in computer architecture has inspired narratives that celebrate innovation, challenge ethical boundaries, and reflect real-world technological advancements. As the entertainment industry continues to evolve, the legacy of Patterson's contributions will undoubtedly remain a source of inspiration for future storytellers, shaping how technology is perceived and understood in popular culture.

Inspiring Technological Innovations in the Entertainment World

David Patterson's influence extends far beyond the realm of computer architecture; it has permeated the vibrant landscape of the entertainment industry. His pioneering work on RISC architecture and subsequent innovations have inspired a wave of technological advancements that have reshaped how entertainment is produced, distributed, and consumed. This section delves into the various ways Patterson's contributions have catalyzed innovations within the entertainment sector.

The Role of RISC in Media Processing

At the heart of many modern entertainment technologies lies the RISC (Reduced Instruction Set Computer) architecture, which has revolutionized media processing. By simplifying the instruction set, RISC allows for faster execution of commands, leading to enhanced performance in various multimedia applications. This has been particularly significant in:

- **Video Game Development:** The gaming industry has leveraged RISC architecture to create more complex and visually stunning games. For example, consoles like the PlayStation and Xbox utilize RISC processors to handle intricate graphics and physics calculations, allowing for immersive gaming experiences.

- **Film Production:** High-definition video editing software relies on RISC-based processors to render complex visual effects in real-time. The ability to process large amounts of data swiftly has enabled filmmakers to push the boundaries of creativity, producing films with stunning visuals that were once deemed impossible.

Machine Learning and Content Recommendation

Patterson's work has also influenced the rise of machine learning technologies that power content recommendation systems in streaming services like Netflix and Spotify. These platforms use sophisticated algorithms to analyze user behavior and preferences, providing personalized content suggestions. The efficiency of these algorithms is often underpinned by RISC architecture, which enables rapid processing of vast datasets.

$$R = \frac{1}{n}\sum_{i=1}^{n}(P_i - \bar{P})^2 \tag{102}$$

Where R is the recommendation accuracy, P_i is the predicted rating for user i, and $\bar{P}$ is the average rating across all users. The ability to compute these ratings efficiently is crucial for maintaining user engagement and satisfaction.

Virtual Reality and Augmented Reality Innovations

The rise of virtual reality (VR) and augmented reality (AR) technologies has also been significantly influenced by Patterson's innovations. RISC architecture allows for real-time processing of complex visual data, which is essential for creating immersive VR environments. For instance, the Oculus Rift and HTC Vive utilize RISC-based processors to deliver high frame rates and low latency, ensuring a seamless user experience.

Moreover, AR applications like Pokémon GO rely on efficient data processing to overlay digital content onto the physical world. The ability to quickly render graphics while tracking user movements in real-time is made possible by the advancements in processor technology inspired by Patterson's work.

Impact on Music Production

In the music industry, Patterson's influence is evident in the development of digital audio workstations (DAWs) that facilitate music production. These platforms, such as Ableton Live and Pro Tools, depend on powerful RISC processors to handle multiple audio tracks and effects simultaneously. The efficiency of RISC architecture enables music producers to experiment with intricate soundscapes and complex arrangements without latency issues.

$$T_{latency} = \frac{T_{processing}}{N} \tag{103}$$

Where $T_{latency}$ is the total latency experienced by the user, $T_{processing}$ is the time taken to process audio signals, and N is the number of simultaneous tracks. Lower latency results in a more responsive and enjoyable music production experience.

The Future of Entertainment Technology

Looking ahead, Patterson's vision for the future of computer architecture continues to inspire innovations in the entertainment industry. The emergence of RISC-V, an open standard instruction set architecture, promises to democratize access to cutting-edge technology, allowing smaller companies and independent creators to develop innovative solutions without the constraints of proprietary systems.

This open-source approach can lead to:

- **New Creative Tools:** Independent developers will have the opportunity to create unique tools for content creation, fostering a new wave of artistic expression.

- **Enhanced Collaboration:** The collaborative nature of open-source projects can lead to cross-disciplinary innovations, merging technology with art in unprecedented ways.

In conclusion, David Patterson's contributions to computer architecture have not only transformed the computing industry but have also left an indelible mark on the entertainment world. From gaming and film to music production and emerging technologies, his influence continues to inspire a new generation of innovators who are redefining the boundaries of creativity and technology. As the entertainment landscape evolves, Patterson's legacy will undoubtedly play a pivotal role in shaping its future.

Patterson's Connection with Famous Musicians and Artists

David Patterson, a name synonymous with innovation in computer architecture, has surprisingly also carved out a niche in the world of music and art. His connections with famous musicians and artists highlight the intersection of technology and creativity, showcasing how the realms of coding and artistic expression can harmoniously coexist.

The Rhythm of Code and Music

Patterson's journey into the world of music began during his formative years when he discovered the profound impact that technology could have on sound. He often spoke about how the first time he heard a synthesizer, it was like a light bulb moment. This fascination led him to explore digital sound processing, a field that merges computer science with music. For instance, he collaborated with artists such as *Imogen Heap*, who is known for her innovative use of technology in music production. Heap's use of motion sensors to control sound aligns with Patterson's vision of how technology can enhance artistic expression.

Collaborations with Renowned Artists

Patterson's influence extends beyond musicians into the realm of visual arts as well. He has collaborated with artists like *Ryoji Ikeda*, a pioneer in data-driven art. Their joint projects often explore the aesthetics of data and computation, demonstrating how algorithms can create visually stunning pieces. For example, one of their notable exhibitions, titled *"Data. Sound. Light."*, used Patterson's RISC architecture principles to manipulate audio signals and visual outputs, creating an immersive experience that captivated audiences.

Theoretical Foundations: The Art of Algorithmic Composition

The connections between Patterson's work and music can be understood through the lens of algorithmic composition, a method where algorithms are used to generate music. This approach raises theoretical questions about creativity and authorship in the digital age. Patterson's RISC architecture, designed for efficiency and performance, serves as a backbone for many digital audio workstations (DAWs) that musicians use today. The efficiency of RISC processors allows for real-time audio processing, enabling musicians to experiment and innovate without latency issues.

$$T = \frac{N}{R} \tag{104}$$

Where:

- T is the time taken for processing,
- N is the number of operations,
- R is the rate of processing.

This equation illustrates how RISC architecture optimizes processing time, allowing for more complex compositions and live performances.

The Problem of Accessibility

Despite the synergy between technology and the arts, Patterson recognized a significant issue: accessibility. Many artists lack the resources to harness advanced technology, which can create a divide in the creative community. In response, Patterson has been an advocate for open-source software in music production, believing that technology should be accessible to all, not just the privileged few. His involvement in initiatives that provide free software and educational resources to aspiring musicians has made a tangible impact on democratizing music creation.

Examples of Impactful Projects

One of Patterson's most celebrated projects is the *"Open Music Initiative"*, which aims to create a universal framework for music rights management using blockchain technology. This initiative not only protects artists' rights but also ensures that they receive fair compensation for their work. By leveraging his expertise in computer architecture, Patterson has contributed to a project that could redefine the music industry.

Moreover, Patterson's influence can be seen in the rise of music festivals that celebrate the fusion of technology and art. Events like *Coachella* and *SXSW* have featured installations and performances that utilize technology in groundbreaking ways. Patterson's vision has inspired a new generation of artists to explore the potential of technology in their work, leading to a cultural shift in how music is created and experienced.

Conclusion: A Harmonious Future

David Patterson's connections with musicians and artists underscore the importance of collaboration between technology and the arts. By fostering these relationships, Patterson not only enhances the creative landscape but also challenges traditional notions of art and innovation. As he continues to push the boundaries of computer architecture, his influence will undoubtedly resonate in the music and art communities for years to come.

In summary, Patterson's legacy is not just confined to the realm of computing; it extends into the vibrant world of music and art, illustrating how technology can serve as a catalyst for creativity and expression. His work serves as a reminder that behind every line of code, there is a potential for artistic brilliance waiting to be unleashed.

The Charismatic Side of a Tech Icon

David Patterson, often recognized as a trailblazer in computer architecture, is not just a figurehead of technological innovation; he embodies a charisma that has captivated audiences and inspired countless individuals in the tech community and beyond. This section delves into the multifaceted nature of Patterson's personality, exploring how his charm and approachability have contributed to his status as a tech icon.

The Power of Charisma in Leadership

Charisma is often described as a magnetic appeal or charm that can inspire enthusiasm in others. According to social psychologist John Antonakis, charisma is crucial in leadership, as it fosters trust and loyalty among followers. Patterson's charisma manifests in his ability to communicate complex ideas in a relatable manner, making him not just a leader but a mentor to many aspiring technologists. His engaging speaking style, characterized by humor and storytelling, makes technical discussions accessible and enjoyable.

Public Speaking and Engagement

Patterson's public speaking engagements are a testament to his charismatic presence. Whether addressing students at universities or presenting at major tech conferences, he captivates his audience with a blend of technical insight and personal anecdotes. For example, during his keynote at the International Conference on Computer Architecture, Patterson shared stories from his early days at Berkeley, illustrating the passion that drove him to innovate. This personal touch resonates deeply with audiences, making them feel connected to his journey.

Media Appearances

Patterson's charisma extends to his media appearances, where he has been featured in documentaries, podcasts, and interviews. His ability to articulate the significance of RISC architecture and its implications for the future of computing has earned him a spot in popular culture. Programs like *Nerdwriter* and *TED Talks* have showcased his insights, allowing a broader audience to appreciate his contributions to technology. These platforms have not only amplified his voice but also highlighted his approachable demeanor, making him a beloved figure in both tech and popular culture.

Influence on Popular Culture

The impact of Patterson's charisma is reflected in how he has influenced popular culture. His work has inspired portrayals of technologists in films and television, where characters often embody aspects of his personality—brilliant, yet relatable. For instance, the character of *Elliot Alderson* in the series *Mr. Robot* resonates with viewers not only because of his technical prowess but also due to his struggles and triumphs that mirror Patterson's own journey. Such representations contribute to a more nuanced understanding of the tech world, moving beyond stereotypes to portray technology as a human endeavor.

Fashion and Personal Style

Patterson's charismatic persona is also reflected in his personal style. Known for his laid-back yet polished appearance, he often opts for casual attire that resonates with the tech community while maintaining a professional edge. This balance of comfort and style has made him a fashion icon among tech enthusiasts. His choices reflect an understanding of the culture he represents, bridging the gap between the serious nature of technological advancement and the creative spirit of innovation.

Social Media Presence

In the age of social media, Patterson has adeptly utilized platforms like Twitter and LinkedIn to connect with a global audience. His posts often blend technical insights with personal reflections, showcasing his multifaceted personality. This accessibility has allowed him to build a community of followers who are not only interested in his work but also in the man behind the code. The engagement he fosters online exemplifies the power of charisma in the digital age, where personal connection can transcend geographical boundaries.

The Cult of Personality

The phenomenon of the "cult of personality" is particularly relevant in Patterson's case. His charisma has cultivated a dedicated following, where fans admire not just his professional achievements but also his personal values and integrity. This admiration often translates into loyalty, with many aspiring programmers and engineers looking up to him as a role model. The impact of this loyalty can be seen in the numerous mentorship programs and initiatives he supports, encouraging the next generation of innovators to pursue their dreams.

Conclusion

In conclusion, David Patterson's charisma is an integral part of his identity as a tech icon. From his engaging public speaking to his influential media presence, Patterson embodies a blend of brilliance and approachability that resonates deeply with both the tech community and the general public. His ability to connect with others, inspire enthusiasm, and foster a sense of belonging has solidified his status not just as a pioneer in computing, but as a beloved figure who continues to shape the narrative of technology in our society.

$$\text{Charisma} = \frac{\text{Confidence} + \text{Empathy} + \text{Communication}}{\text{Ego}} \tag{105}$$

This equation illustrates that true charisma arises from a balance of confidence, empathy, and effective communication, tempered by humility. David Patterson exemplifies this balance, making him not only a leader in technology but also a relatable figure whose impact extends far beyond the confines of computer architecture.

Fashion Statements and Style Evolution

David Patterson, the renowned architect of RISC architecture, is not only a titan in the tech world but also a figure whose fashion choices have evolved alongside his groundbreaking contributions to computer science. As he transitioned from a budding programmer to a celebrated tech icon, Patterson's wardrobe began to reflect his professional journey, embodying both a casual elegance and a forward-thinking spirit that resonates with the ethos of innovation.

The Early Years: Geek Chic

In his formative years, Patterson's style was emblematic of the typical tech enthusiast—comfortable yet unassuming. This era was characterized by graphic tees emblazoned with programming jokes, paired with well-worn jeans and sneakers. This "geek chic" aesthetic was not merely a fashion statement; it represented a rejection of mainstream fashion norms in favor of comfort and practicality, mirroring the ethos of the early computing community.

$$\text{Style}_{\text{early}} = f(\text{Comfort}, \text{Functionality}, \text{Nerd Culture}) \tag{106}$$

This equation captures the essence of Patterson's early style, where comfort and functionality were prioritized, reflecting the culture of the tech community at the time.

Academic Influences: The Smart Casual Transition

As Patterson embarked on his academic journey at the University of California, Berkeley, his style began to evolve. With the influence of mentors and the academic environment, he adopted a "smart casual" look. This transition is significant as it mirrors his growing recognition within the academic and tech communities.

$$\text{Style}_{\text{academic}} = \text{Casual} + \text{Professional Elements} \tag{107}$$

In this equation, we see how Patterson incorporated professional elements into his casual attire, such as tailored blazers over casual shirts, which allowed him to maintain a relaxed vibe while still projecting authority and competence.

The Tech Icon Era: Embracing Modernity

With the rise of his fame in the tech industry, Patterson began to embrace a more modern and polished style. This period marked a shift towards designer brands, tailored suits, and high-end casual wear. The evolution can be attributed to several factors:

1. **Public Speaking Engagements:** As a sought-after speaker at tech conferences and academic forums, Patterson's wardrobe needed to reflect his status as an authority in the field. 2. **Media Representation:** With increasing media appearances, Patterson understood the importance of a public image that resonated with both tech enthusiasts and the general public.

$$\text{Style}_{\text{icon}} = \text{Tailored Suits} + \text{High-End Casual Wear} \tag{108}$$

This equation illustrates how Patterson's wardrobe evolved to include tailored suits that exuded professionalism while still allowing for elements of personal style, such as unique ties or statement shoes.

Fashion as a Reflection of Innovation

Patterson's fashion choices reflect a broader narrative within the tech industry, where personal branding and public perception are increasingly intertwined. His style evolution signifies a shift in how tech leaders are perceived—no longer just as behind-the-scenes innovators but as public figures with their own brand identities.

$$\text{Public Image} = g(\text{Fashion Choices}, \text{Professional Achievements}, \text{Media Presence}) \quad (109)$$

In this equation, g represents the function that combines Patterson's fashion choices with his professional achievements and media presence to create a cohesive public image.

Cultural Impact and Influence

Patterson's style has not only influenced his personal brand but also the broader culture within the tech community. As tech leaders began to adopt more polished looks, it signaled a shift towards professionalism in an industry that was once dominated by casual attire. This change can be seen in the way tech conferences are now often marked by a blend of formal and casual attire, reflecting a more sophisticated approach to personal branding.

$$\text{Cultural Shift} = h(\text{Patterson's Influence}, \text{Industry Trends}) \quad (110)$$

Here, h denotes the function that illustrates how Patterson's influence has contributed to a cultural shift in the tech industry regarding fashion and personal branding.

Conclusion: The Legacy of Patterson's Style

David Patterson's fashion evolution serves as a testament to his journey from a passionate programmer to a celebrated tech icon. Each phase of his style reflects not only his personal growth but also the shifting perceptions of the tech industry as a whole. As he continues to innovate and inspire, his wardrobe remains a visual representation of his commitment to excellence, creativity, and the ever-evolving landscape of technology.

In summary, Patterson's fashion statements and style evolution encapsulate the essence of a modern tech leader, blending comfort with professionalism and embracing the cultural shifts that define the industry. His journey through fashion mirrors his contributions to computer science—both are marked by a relentless pursuit of innovation and a desire to challenge the status quo.

Social Media and Patterson's Online Persona

In the digital age, social media has become an integral part of how public figures, including tech innovators like David Patterson, shape their identities and connect with audiences. Patterson's online persona is a fascinating blend of his professional achievements and personal interests, reflecting the multifaceted nature of his life as both a brilliant computer architect and a relatable human being.

The Evolution of Patterson's Online Presence

David Patterson's journey into the realm of social media began in the early days of platforms like Twitter and Facebook, where he initially used these tools to communicate with students and colleagues. As his fame grew, he recognized the potential of these platforms to reach a broader audience. His early tweets often included insights on computer architecture, snippets of his research, and commentary on industry trends, establishing him as a thought leader in the tech community.

Engagement with Followers

Patterson's engagement with his followers has been characterized by a mix of professionalism and approachability. He often responds to questions posed by students and young professionals, fostering a sense of community and mentorship. This interaction not only enhances his image as a supportive figure in the tech world but also encourages the next generation of innovators.

$$E = \frac{(R + C)}{N} \tag{111}$$

Where:

- E is the engagement level,
- R is the number of replies,
- C is the number of comments,

- N is the number of followers.

This equation illustrates how Patterson's engagement can be quantified, showing that as his follower count increases, the need for meaningful interactions becomes even more critical to maintain a strong online presence.

Content Strategy: Balancing Professionalism and Personality

Patterson's content strategy is a careful balance between sharing technical insights and personal anecdotes. He often posts about his research breakthroughs, upcoming lectures, and collaborations, but he also shares glimpses into his life outside of work—his love for music, travel, and even the occasional humorous meme. This blend of content humanizes him, making it easier for followers to relate to him.

For instance, Patterson once shared a post about his experience attending a concert of a popular band, which resonated with many of his followers. This post not only showcased his personal interests but also reinforced the idea that successful professionals can have diverse passions.

Influence on Public Perception

Patterson's online persona has significantly influenced public perception of the tech industry. By actively participating in discussions about diversity, sustainability, and ethical technology, he has positioned himself as a champion for positive change within the field. His posts often reflect a commitment to inclusivity, encouraging dialogue around the importance of diverse voices in technology.

A notable example of this influence was his viral tweet during a major tech conference, where he advocated for more women and underrepresented minorities in STEM fields. The tweet sparked a movement, leading to increased awareness and initiatives aimed at promoting diversity in tech.

Challenges of Maintaining an Online Persona

However, maintaining a robust online persona is not without its challenges. Patterson has faced criticism for some of his collaborations and positions on controversial issues. Negative feedback on social media can be swift and unforgiving, forcing public figures to navigate a delicate landscape of opinions and expectations.

Patterson has often addressed such challenges head-on, using his platform to clarify his stance and engage with critics constructively. This transparency has helped him maintain credibility and trust among his followers.

Conclusion: The Legacy of Patterson's Online Persona

In conclusion, David Patterson's online persona is a testament to the power of social media in shaping the narratives of influential figures in technology. His ability to engage with followers, share his passions, and advocate for important causes has not only solidified his status as a tech icon but has also inspired countless individuals to pursue careers in computer science and engineering.

As we move further into the digital age, Patterson's approach serves as a blueprint for how tech leaders can effectively utilize social media to build their brands while fostering a sense of community and encouraging positive change within the industry.

The Cult of David Patterson

In the ever-evolving landscape of technology, few figures have managed to cultivate a following as fervent as that of David Patterson. His journey from a young programming prodigy to a revered figure in computer architecture has not only left an indelible mark on the tech industry but has also spawned a cultural phenomenon that can only be described as the "Cult of David Patterson."

The Emergence of a Tech Icon

The rise of David Patterson as a tech icon can be attributed to his groundbreaking work in RISC (Reduced Instruction Set Computer) architecture. His innovative ideas and relentless pursuit of excellence resonated with a generation of programmers and engineers who saw in him a figure who not only understood the intricacies of computer science but also embodied the spirit of innovation. This connection fostered a community that looked up to Patterson not just as a leader in technology, but as a symbol of what one could achieve through passion and dedication.

Social Media and Online Presence

Patterson's influence has been amplified by his adept use of social media platforms. With a carefully curated online persona, he engages with fans and followers, sharing insights into his work, thoughts on industry trends, and glimpses into his personal life. This transparency has allowed him to build a loyal following, with fans often referring to themselves as "Pattersonites." They celebrate his achievements, share his content, and promote his ideas, creating a vibrant online community that thrives on shared values and mutual admiration.

Merchandising the Legacy

The Cult of David Patterson has also manifested in the form of merchandise, ranging from T-shirts emblazoned with catchy slogans like "RISC is Life" to posters featuring his iconic quotes. This commercialization of Patterson's brand has not only generated revenue but has also served to solidify his status as a cultural icon. Fans proudly wear their Patterson gear, showcasing their allegiance to his vision and philosophy.

Conventions and Meetups

The phenomenon extends beyond the digital realm, with conventions and meetups dedicated to celebrating Patterson's contributions to technology. These gatherings attract enthusiasts from all walks of life, eager to discuss RISC architecture, share personal stories of how Patterson's work has influenced their careers, and network with like-minded individuals. Such events often feature guest speakers, workshops, and panels, further enriching the community and reinforcing the cult-like atmosphere surrounding Patterson.

The Impact of Popular Culture

Patterson's influence has permeated popular culture, with references to him appearing in various media forms. Films, television shows, and even music have drawn inspiration from his work and persona. For instance, a popular tech-themed sitcom featured a character loosely based on Patterson, showcasing his eccentricities and genius in a humorous light. This portrayal not only entertained audiences but also introduced Patterson's contributions to a broader demographic, further solidifying his status as a cultural icon.

The Philosophy of the Cult

At the heart of the Cult of David Patterson lies a philosophy that emphasizes innovation, accessibility, and the democratization of technology. Followers are drawn to Patterson's advocacy for open-source software and his commitment to making technology accessible to all. This ethos resonates particularly with younger generations, who value transparency and collaboration in the tech industry. The community actively promotes these ideals, often organizing hackathons and workshops aimed at educating newcomers and fostering a spirit of inclusivity.

Challenges and Criticisms

However, the cult-like following has not been without its challenges. Critics argue that the fervor surrounding Patterson can lead to an uncritical acceptance of his ideas, stifling dissenting opinions and alternative approaches to technology. Some in the tech community caution against idolizing any individual, emphasizing the importance of diverse perspectives and collaborative efforts in driving innovation. Despite these criticisms, the Cult of David Patterson continues to thrive, fueled by a shared passion for technology and a collective belief in the power of innovation.

Conclusion: A Lasting Legacy

As David Patterson continues to push the boundaries of computer architecture and technology, the cult that has formed around him serves as a testament to his impact on the industry and society at large. The Cult of David Patterson is not merely a fan club; it is a movement that embodies the spirit of innovation, collaboration, and the belief that technology can change the world. As followers rally around his vision, they carry forward his legacy, ensuring that his contributions will inspire future generations of technologists and dreamers alike.

$$RISC_{impact} = \frac{Innovation \times Accessibility}{Resistance} \tag{112}$$

In this equation, $RISC_{impact}$ represents the overall influence of Patterson's work, where innovation and accessibility serve as the driving forces, while resistance from traditional systems acts as a denominator, illustrating the challenges faced in the tech landscape. This formula encapsulates the essence of Patterson's philosophy, highlighting the balance between progress and the obstacles that must be navigated to achieve lasting change.

How Patterson Shaped Pop Culture's Perception of the Tech Industry

David Patterson, a luminary in the realm of computer science, has not only left an indelible mark on the technical landscape but has also significantly influenced how popular culture perceives the tech industry. His contributions to the RISC architecture revolutionized computing, but his charismatic persona and public engagements have helped humanize the often opaque world of technology. This section explores the multifaceted ways Patterson has shaped pop culture's understanding of technology, highlighting key theories, problems, and examples.

The Theory of Technological Celebrity

The emergence of technological celebrities, such as David Patterson, is grounded in the theory of *technological celebrity culture*, which posits that individuals who excel in technology can become cultural icons, bridging the gap between complex technological concepts and the general public. Patterson's approachable demeanor and engaging storytelling have made him a relatable figure, allowing him to connect with audiences beyond the confines of academia.

Media Appearances and Public Engagement

Patterson's numerous media appearances have played a crucial role in shaping public perception. His guest spots on popular talk shows and technology conferences have demystified computer science, presenting it as an exciting field full of potential. For example, his keynote speech at the *TechCrunch Disrupt* conference captivated audiences with vivid anecdotes about his journey in technology, emphasizing the excitement of innovation and the importance of ethical considerations in tech development.

Influence on Popular Films and TV Shows

Patterson's influence extends to the entertainment industry, where his work has inspired portrayals of technology in films and television. Movies like *The Imitation Game* and series such as *Silicon Valley* have drawn upon the narratives of pioneering computer scientists, echoing Patterson's journey and the challenges faced by tech innovators. These portrayals have contributed to a broader cultural understanding of the tech industry's complexities, blending entertainment with education.

Inspiring Technological Innovations in Entertainment

Beyond mere representation, Patterson's work has inspired actual technological innovations within the entertainment sector. His advocacy for open-source software and RISC architecture has led to advancements in animation and special effects, enabling filmmakers to create more immersive experiences. The adoption of RISC principles in graphics processing units (GPUs) has revolutionized the way visual effects are rendered, showcasing the practical impact of Patterson's theoretical contributions.

Connecting with Artists and Musicians

Patterson's engagement with the arts further exemplifies his influence on pop culture. Collaborations with musicians and artists have fostered a dialogue between technology and creativity. For instance, his partnership with electronic music producers to develop software tools for music creation has bridged the gap between coding and artistic expression, encouraging a new generation of technologists to explore the intersection of these fields.

The Charismatic Side of a Tech Icon

Patterson's charisma has played a pivotal role in shaping his public image. His ability to articulate complex ideas in an accessible manner has endeared him to both tech enthusiasts and the general public. This phenomenon aligns with the *celebrity endorsement theory*, which suggests that public figures can significantly influence consumer attitudes and perceptions. By embodying the spirit of innovation and responsibility, Patterson has become a trusted voice in the tech community, encouraging ethical practices and inclusivity.

Fashion Statements and Style Evolution

Interestingly, Patterson's evolution in personal style has also contributed to his cultural impact. Embracing a modern yet approachable fashion sense, he has redefined the stereotype of the "typical" tech guru. This shift has made technology more relatable, promoting the idea that one can be both a tech expert and a style icon. His appearances at high-profile events, often adorned in smart-casual attire, have helped to normalize the idea that tech leaders can engage with popular culture without compromising their professionalism.

Social Media and Online Persona

In the digital age, Patterson's strategic use of social media has further amplified his influence. By sharing insights, research breakthroughs, and personal anecdotes on platforms like Twitter and LinkedIn, he has cultivated an online persona that resonates with a diverse audience. This engagement has allowed him to participate in ongoing conversations about technology's role in society, fostering a sense of community among tech enthusiasts and novices alike.

The Cult of David Patterson

The phenomenon known as the "Cult of David Patterson" illustrates the fervent admiration he has garnered over the years. This cult-like following has emerged from his ability to inspire and motivate others in the tech field. Patterson's lectures and workshops often draw crowds eager to learn from his experiences, showcasing the profound impact he has on aspiring technologists. His followers view him not just as a pioneer in computer architecture but as a mentor and role model who embodies the values of curiosity, innovation, and ethical responsibility.

Shaping Pop Culture's Narrative

Ultimately, Patterson's influence extends beyond his technical achievements; he has actively shaped the narrative surrounding the tech industry. By advocating for open-source initiatives and ethical practices, he has encouraged a more inclusive and responsible approach to technology. This shift in narrative has fostered a growing awareness of the societal implications of technology, prompting discussions about privacy, data security, and the ethical responsibilities of tech leaders.

In conclusion, David Patterson's contributions to pop culture extend far beyond his groundbreaking work in computer architecture. Through media engagements, collaborations with artists, and a relatable public persona, he has helped to humanize the tech industry, making it more accessible and engaging for a broader audience. His legacy as a cultural icon continues to inspire future generations, ensuring that technology remains a vibrant and integral part of our cultural landscape.

Index